The **8** Proven Secrets to SMART Success

Peggy McColl

www.destinies.com
Destinies Publishing
1 Stafford Road, Suite 312
Nepean, Ontario K2H 1B9
(613) 299-5722

ISBN 0-9730431-2-1
Printed and bound in Canada
©2002 Peggy McColl

Editing by Janet Shorten
Cover design by Fernando Martinez, 3dA Multimedia Inc.

Production by Destinies Publishing
        Marie Tappin, Text Design

Printing number 10 9 8 7 6 5 4 3 2 1

National Library of Canada Cataloguing in Publication Data

McColl, Peggy
        The 8 proven secrets to SMART success / Peggy McColl; editing by Janet Shorten.

Includes bibliographical references
ISBN 0-9730431-2-1

        1. Self-realization. 2. Success. I. Shorten, Janet II. Title. III. Title: Eight proven secrets to SMART success.

BF637.S8M336 2002   158.1   C2002-905850-3

Endorsements for *The 8 Proven Secrets to SMART Success*

● ● ● ● ● ● ● ●

"Anyone who will follow the blueprint outlined in this book will meet with uncommon success. I urge you to take the journey."
– Jack Canfield, co-author of the *Chicken Soup for the Soul*® series, *Dare to Win* and *The Power of Focus: How to Hit All Your Business, Personal and Financial Targets with Absolute Certainty.*

"Here is a book that will help you create an extraordinary life. Peggy McColl provides powerful secrets that produce amazing results. Put Peggy's ideas into action today and watch your life transform."
– Robert Stuberg, founder and Chairman of Success.com, author of *The 12 Life Secrets* and *Creating Your Ultimate Destiny.*

"I have known Peggy McColl for years. She is an amazing woman who has spent years developing herself. Then, with magical precision, she was ready and took off like a rocket. Happiness, Health and Wealth are her reward and just keep flowing her way. This lady is powerful and her information should be taught in schools. The Good Life and the way to achieve it is clearly outlined between the covers of this book."
—Bob Proctor, author of *You Were Born Rich*

"Read this book! Peggy will share with you the secrets that could very possibly propel you into extraordinary abundance."
—Mark Victor Hansen, co-creator, #1 New York Times best-selling series *Chicken Soup for the Soul*®, and co-author, *The One Minute Millionaire*

● ● ● ● ● ● ● ●

"The *8 Proven Secrets to SMART Success* raises the barrier beyond that which was ever written on the subject. The simplicity and clarity of its messages can only be compared to the Book of Life. I call this book The Success Bible!"
—William E. Bailey, Horatio Alger Award recipient

"This is the SMARTEST book on success you will ever get your hands on."
—Jim Rohn, author of the best-selling book *The 5 Major Pieces to the Life Puzzle*

"With *The 8 Proven Secrets to SMART Success*, Peggy McColl is now right up there with some of the greatest personal development authors in the world. She has expertly distilled the 'Laws of the Universe' from years and years of research and personal application. More importantly, she has compiled that wisdom in a unique and easy-to-follow style that allows anyone else to apply the Laws as well. This information is exciting to learn. As you read each golden-nugget-filled page, you'll be glad you decided to own this book. Get your highlighter and pen out. You'll take lots of notes, and be all the 'richer' for it."
– Bob Burg, author of *Winning Without Intimidation, Endless Referrals* and *GOSSIP: Ten Pathways to Eliminate It from Your Life and Transform Your Soul*

"Peggy McColl has created a wondrous book! The kind of book you will buy in quantity because you will want to use the copies for gifts to people you really care about. How could you give a better gift than her *8 Proven Secrets to SMART Success*? Well done, Peggy!"
—Dottie Walters, author of *Speak and Grow Rich*, President/CEO of Walters International Speakers Bureau, publisher of *Sharing Ideas*, International Speakers' Magazine

"Achieving success will no longer be a secret after you read and apply the proven principles found in Peggy's book."
– Cynthia Kersey, author of *Unstoppable*

● ● ● ● ● ● ● ●

Dedication

To Bob Proctor,
a great Master,
a great friend

Acknowledgments

· · · · · · · ·

Michel Poulin, my son, my priority! Thank you for your youth, your inspiration and your valuable suggestions. You have wisdom far beyond your years. You are truly loved and appreciated.

My great and wondrous team player, Debbie Heika. Ready, willing and contributing at the highest level at all hours, any time, any day. Debbie is a gift to my business and a great friend in my life. Thank you for your unwavering support and kindness.

Enormous thanks for two incredible beings, Bob and Linda Proctor. Bob, to whom this book is dedicated, has been my greatest mentor and has had the most profound impact on my growth. There are no words that could possibly express my overflowing gratitude. And, for Linda, who so willingly and graciously accepted my request to write the foreword for this book, only to provide the most moving and inspiring foreword that any author could ever ask for. Thank you both.

A sincere thank you to Gina Hayden for keeping the connection with the Proctors and, with all of our busy schedules, I really appreciate your following through when I really needed you.

To my special friend William E. Bailey, who has an amazing style unlike any other. So full of wisdom and inspiration that I am blessed to know you, and privileged to call you a friend.

· · · · · · · ·

Joe Vitale, a great friend and support and one of the most talented marketing minds of our generation. Thank you, Joe, for always being there to help, for offering your incredibly powerful ideas, and for being so kind.

To Trudy Marschall, who is kind, respectful, a great friend, professional and always comes through for me. Thank you for pulling the rabbits out of the hats. You are so appreciated.

Dottie Walters, a new and special friend. You are a great support and so full of knowledge and wisdom and so willing to share.

Jerry Jenkins, you have become a great mentor, but more importantly, a great friend. Thank you for all of your support, contact information, and sharing your wealth of knowledge of the book industry.

Thank you for Mark Victor Hansen, Jack Canfield, Robert Stuberg, Cynthia Kersey, Jim Rohn and Bob Burg for coming through with the most wonderful endorsements and for showing your support and care.

To Tami DePalma, thank you for being such an incredibly talented marketing sensation! And, more importantly, thank you for your friendship and your energy.

And a huge heartfelt thank you to all of the wonderful people who have helped me with my online promotions for my books and products: David Riklan, Steve Goodier, Mike Litman and Kevin Eikenberry.

A special thanks to Christopher Reeve for his incredible determination and inspiration.

Janet Shorten, the greatest Editor an author could ever dream to work with. I am your biggest fan! Thank you for putting your soul into your work. It truly shows through in everything you do. You are an amazing woman.

● ● ● ● ● ● ● ●

Fernando Martinez, an incredibly talented man and one of my favorite people on the planet. You will never know how much I value you for being who you are and for all that you do for me and my business.

To my special and cherished friends Paul Montelongo, Brenda Moss, Judith Yaworsky, Colleen Moore, Barry Doucette, Hayden Marcus, Shane Belceto, Sandy Laneville, Craig Senior, Diane Craig, Charles Poulin and Anick Lavoie thank you for your warmth, friendship, love and your incredible support.

With great appreciation, love and gratitude, I deeply thank my family for their love, support and thoughtfulness. My Sister Judy McColl, my Mom Rita McColl, my Dad Bob McColl, my Brother Bob McColl and Sister-in-law Alice McColl, and all of my wonderful and loving nieces and nephews: Julie Koster, Steven McColl, Jennifer Lusk, Melissa McColl, Amy Lusk, James McColl, Joshua Lusk and Malik McColl.

And, my Brother Gary McColl, we love you and miss you dearly.

• • • • • • • •

Table of Contents

● ● ● ● ● ● ● ●

● ● ● ● ● ● ● ●

Foreword by Linda Proctor

**To travel hopefully is a better thing than to arrive,
and the true success is to labor.**
– Robert Louis Stevenson

● ● ● ● ● ● ● ●

True success is in the journey and every step of the way can and should be enjoyed. All the great teachers have told us this time and time again. However, too often we are in such a rush to arrive that we miss the joy of life. Many years after Robert Louis Stevenson shared those words of wisdom with us, Earl Nightingale gave us his definition of success, which is strikingly similar to Stevenson's. Mr. Nightingale said, "Success is the progressive realization of a worthy ideal."

As you travel through the pages of this book you will realize that Peggy McColl has learned this lesson well. I have had the pleasure of knowing Peggy for many years now. In *The 8 Proven Secrets to SMART Success* Peggy has done an excellent job in capturing the essential elements to success and sharing them in an organized and cohesive manner. The information you need for greater success is here. Peggy is able to do that because she has done and continues to do that in her own life . . . always challenging herself to reach greater heights . . . always studying to improve herself and her ability to communicate these ideas.

● ● ● ● ● ● ● ●

Before reading this book, think about how you are presently living. Think about how you would like to be living. Make a written description of that mental image and as you read and study this book I challenge you to do two things.

1. Keep that written description of how you would like to be living in front of you. Then use the information as a springboard for ideas that you can implement that will move you closer to your goal.

2. Look for one or two things that you will commit to implementing right now. Things you are not presently doing on a consistent basis. Things you know will make a difference in your life and the results you want.

Twenty-four years ago I met a man who challenged me to do exactly that: set a goal and then commit to two results-producing activities every day. I did, and my results changed dramatically and in a very short period of time. Implementing just two or three ideas from this book will do that for you.

Let Peggy mentor and coach you though the information in this book . . . leading you to greater levels of success in all areas of your life. The results you are now dreaming of achieving can come very quickly with the right information, the right mentors and the right action. You must commit to that action now.

• • • • • • • •

Introduction

● ● ● ● ● ● ● ●

Welcome to *The 8 Proven Secrets to SMART Success.*

This is a special book that takes the best of what I've learned over the last 25 years, from the most successful people, and the essence of what I've had the privilege to share with thousands of people all over the world, and give it to you. This book is an affirmation of the message I have been sharing through my seminars, speaking engagements and other books.

What I have discovered from this near quarter-century of passionate study is that there are very specific things that successful people do, not only to achieve high levels of success, but to create a totally fulfilling life where, in addition to *having* success, they *enjoy* it.

Is that a place where you would like to be? To be able to easily turn your dreams into reality? To become truly successful in every way, and be completely joyful?

I trust the answer for you is a resounding "yes"!

This book might have more aptly been called "The 8 Proven Secrets to *Common Sense Success*". . . because it isn't a higher level of intelligence that is required to be successful, as the title of this book may suggest. Rather, it is simply to become aware of these steps to success and implement them in your life on a daily basis.

● ● ● ● ● ● ● ●

This book is loaded with tremendously powerful tools. I promise you that if you will commit yourself to this book and read each chapter, and implement these strategies, you'll find a complete transformation in your life and become totally successful.

Success can be simple. Success is straightforward. I believe many people do not strive for success because they believe it is complicated. It is NOT complicated! People are simply unaware. It is with awareness that the journey begins. And it is with application that the transformation takes place.

But we can't apply knowledge unless we understand it. That's why this formula is true:

Knowledge + understanding = wisdom

And when we add the ingredient of application (applying what we know), the result is transformation.

Wisdom + application = transformation

You will find as you go through this book that you will be re-introduced to strategies that you may already be familiar with. As Oliver Wendell Holmes said, "We all need an education in the obvious."

These strategies may be simply delivered in a new way, or a different way, but the fundamentals of success haven't changed – they are the same today as they were one hundred years ago.

In addition, there is not a select group of individuals that are chosen to be successful. It is your birthright, just as it is that of the person working in the next cubicle or living next door. You have the power within you to do great things. You have the ability to accomplish any goal that you set for yourself.

● ● ● ● ● ● ● ●

My recommendation, before we go any further, is to decide right here, right now, . . . to become the best that you can be. To truly go within and draw out the best of who you are. Not who you want to be, but who, at your essence, you already are.

Commit to show the world the greatness that is within you. It IS within you. You may not have been aware of this in the past.

Or you were aware that there is greatness within you, but you just haven't demonstrated it to the world.

Choosing to Be Successful
The difference between extraordinary and ordinary is the little "extra."

You see, you have already demonstrated that you are doing the extra by reading in this book. You are that much further ahead.

Let me tell you one of the reasons that causes people to move forward . . . to strive for success.

It is because they are acting with courage. Fear isn't absent from successful people's lives, but they have learned how to step forward in spite of it.

I once heard the expression "It is better to step forward into growth than to step back into safety." Remember this expression any time that you are feeling fear.

Successful people do not step back into safety. They feel the fear and step forward anyway. When we start to feel discomfort, we are growing. We are challenging ourselves.

Discomfort Is Part of the Process
The first time I left my high-paying corporate position and moved into my own business, I felt a ton of discomfort and I was certainly afraid, but I was committed, and in spite of the fear I forged on. To this day, I have zero regrets.

● ● ● ● ● ● ● ●

The feeling of discomfort comes from a place of not knowing – not knowing what is ahead. But even though we may not know what is in front of us, as we step forward the view becomes greater, and answers are revealed.

Think of a mountain climber. To climb a high, steep mountain may appear to be a huge task, and a mountain climber will likely feel fear, especially if it is the first time he or she is climbing that mountain, or any mountain. But, as she moves forward and upward, the unknown becomes known and the view of what is next, what is in front of her, becomes exposed . . . simply because she chooses to step forward. To take another step, and yet another step, until she reaches her destination.

Stepping forward into growth does not necessarily mean huge leaps . . . it could be small steps, baby steps, taken each and every day. Moving forward slowly, easily, effectively, until one day, there she is, miraculously – ON TOP!

But is it a miracle? No, it was an *intended* result. People don't aimlessly and casually go out for a walk one day and wind up on top of a mountain. Landing on top is part of a plan. Being on stop, staying on top, choosing to go to the top, starts with decision.

This book is the beginning of a new journey for you into the greatest quality of life that you've ever imagined.

You've already made a decision to invest in this book, which is an investment in yourself.

And, now let's step forward to reveal the first proven Secret to SMART Success.

● ● ● ● ● ● ● ●

Secret Number 1:
Be Aware

• • • • • • • •

The first Proven Secret to SMART Success is:

BE AWARE

Be aware of your creative power, as you are a creative being.

Be aware of your choices, because they do affect your results.

Be aware of your conscious thoughts, as they are just like seeds that you plant in the ground. They are the starting point to all things.

Be aware of opportunities, because they are everywhere.

Be aware of your beliefs, because they will determine what you are willing to look at and what you will refuse to look at.

I first became aware 25 years ago when I was in prison. No, I wasn't in a physical prison, but I WAS in a psychological prison. What's worse, I had put myself there and didn't even know it.

You see, 25 years ago I attended my first motivational seminar, delivered by a wise and inspiring speaker by the name of Bob Proctor. On that Monday night, as I sat in the front row of the audience, I was struck by one precise message. This one remark changed my life forever.

• • • • • • • •

Bob Proctor said: "You cannot escape from a prison, unless you know you are in one."

This was the point that the light went on. You know what I mean…the light bulb went on above my head and my eyes opened wide, just like in the cartoons. But that was no cartoon.

It was a defining moment. I became aware of my own potential. I became aware of possibilities. I became aware of my inner passion, which was finally ignited.

From that point on was it smooth sailing? As much as I'd like to tell you it was, *it was not.*

Here's what happened. On that life-changing night, I made a commitment to myself —to passionately study personal development and to finally get myself out of my personal pain.

And when Bob Proctor suggested buying books by Napoleon Hill, Dr. Norman Vincent Peale, Norman Cousins, Dr. Maxwell Maltz, Dr. Wayne Dyer – I bought and read all of them. If Bob had an audio program or recommended an audio program, I would buy it and listen to it repeatedly. If he had a "live" seminar coming up, I signed up. I attended his seminars over and over and over again.

It got to a point where I housed more books than most public libraries. I had more audio programs than any recording studio. And here's the irony: my life still wasn't working! I was frustrated.

That was when I decided,

"THIS STUFF DOESN'T WORK!!!!"

●　●　●　●　●　●　●　●

Breaking Through

What did that do? Basically, it removed any of the good that I had just planted in my mind.

I became aware of my own ability to create my results, but what I wasn't aware of was how I was also destroying the good that I was putting in.

Just imagine, if you will, two water glasses on a table in front of you. One glass is full of water and the other glass is full of coffee. Imagine that the glass that is full of water represents a mind that is extremely positive and full of goodness. Imagine the other glass, the one filled with coffee, as a very dark mind that is completely negative.

Imagine what happens when you take a teaspoon of the nice clear water and put a teaspoon of water into the glass that contains the dark coffee. Nothing . . . at least, it appears that nothing is happening. But the fact is, the clear water did go into the glass. We just didn't see any visible result, even though the water was in there.

Basically, the dark coffee was my mind 25 years ago . . . full of negativity. I needed to put in the good (the clear water), and I did just that by feeding my mind with positive material.

If I continue to put teaspoon after teaspoon of water into the glass with the coffee, it will take a long time before you see any measurable difference.

If, on the other hand, you imagine we are starting again with two fresh glasses (one with coffee and one with water) and I took a teaspoon of the coffee and poured it into the glass with the water, would you see a difference? You bet you would. Immediately you would see the impact of placing one teaspoon of coffee into the glass of clear water.

What does this have to do with anything?

● ● ● ● ● ● ● ●

It illustrates the point that when we put good into a mind that is full of negativity, there is a period of time that will elapse before we start to see or experience any change, even though the change is occurring.

On the other hand, when we place just one teaspoon of coffee into the glass of water, the change is instant. This demonstrates the power and velocity of negativity and confirms how fast negativity can contaminate.

Therefore, it is vitally important to be aware of what we are doing when we put good into a negative mind, and to be patient. And it is vitally important to be aware of the negativity (or, as I like to call it, the poison) that we may be putting into our mind, and eliminate it.

Awareness will open your consciousness. Awareness opens your heart and your eyes. You'll see things that you didn't see before . . . things that were right in front of you.

Let me explain further why awareness is so powerful, and so important.

There are two more incentives to become aware:

1. We need to become aware of the things that we do, or have done, that sabotage our own results, so that we can do something about it!

Not so that we can judge ourselves, but so that we can make a decision moving forward to make some positive direction choices. Judgment destroys and accomplishes nothing. Observation (awareness) builds and creates new opportunities. Do not judge your past results; instead, learn from them and move forward. Your future is in front of you . . . look in that direction. Judgment will only hold you back . . . it will make you feel bad . . . it will not support you.

● ● ● ● ● ● ● ●

THE **8** PROVEN SECRETS TO SMART SUCCESS

Being aware of the things that have held you back is like recognizing that there is an anchor weighing you down, keeping you from going forward and experiencing success . . . even when you are on the right course. You've got to cut the anchor rope and let go of these weakening behaviors.

We human beings are habitual creatures, and we tend to do the same things over and over again.

I'm certain you've heard the definition of insanity . . . which is "doing the same thing over and over again and expecting a different result."

These results come from a place of "unaware." Awareness will give the answers.

2. You also need to be aware of the things you are doing that ARE contributing to your success. Why? So you can repeat them if you choose to re-create again or to improve upon your results and continue to enjoy life at a higher level.

Once you achieve great success, it is easy to repeat it because you are now aware of what is required to CREATE success.

Make the choice to be aware and continue to heighten your awareness, not only for today, but from this day forward. Increase your level of awareness as you go through this book. Develop the ability to be acutely aware of all of your creative power and embrace it, utilize it and engage it to create the success that you have previously dreamed of.

So let's begin. In order to receive maximum benefit from this secret, here's what I recommend that you do over the next week.

● ● ● ● ● ● ● ●

Exercise 1

Be aware of what your consistent thoughts are. Be aware of the positive thoughts that you have and the poisonous thoughts that you allow to enter your mind.

Here's how you'll do this:

Take two sheets of paper. On the first sheet of paper, 1A, write down the things you have been doing, the thoughts you have, the disciplines you have developed, the beliefs you have created, the gratitude you feel, the contributions you make, all of which are positive, supportive and do take you in the direction of your goals. Write these down, all of them.

You can begin to write them down now and continue the list whenever you think of more over the next week.

On the second sheet of paper, 1B, write down the thoughts, beliefs, behaviors, disciplines that you have been consistently engaging in that are holding you back from achieving your goals.

This may not seem like a glamorous exercise, but I'm here to tell you this may be the most important exercise you ever do. This will give you the awareness of what has been stopping you from achieving your goals.

Carry these sheets of paper with you and record any additional positive and supportive things, as well as any negative things, that you remember during the week.

Exercise 2

Throughout the week, write down what you would like to get out of this book. Be clear on your outcome. What is your outcome for *The 8 Proven Secrets to SMART Success*? Set the intention for this book right from the start. Get clear on this.

What is it in your life that you would like to change or improve?

● ● ● ● ● ● ● ●

Or are you, also, in a prison that you have decided to escape from?

Exercise 3
Throughout the week, become aware of your dreams.

What dreams do you have deep within you? What are your dreams? Are they waiting to be awakened?

What are you longing for? Simply become aware of this. You don't have to write it down because we will get into this in greater detail in Secret Number 2, but simply become aware and start to shift your focus in this direction.

Awareness is key. If you don't grasp this, the rest of this book will not be as effective. Get this now. Put yourself into this awareness. You've invested in this book: start with awareness and follow through.

Be aware at the highest level and this will propel you to create magic in your own life. It will work. I guarantee it.

> ## "Awareness is to your mind what light is to a darkened room."
> — Peggy McColl

Special Note:
At the conclusion of the first week, here's what I suggest that you do with the results of the first exercise from this section.

AWARENESS EXERCISE SHEET #1A
Positive: What are the things you have been doing, the thoughts you have been thinking, the disciplines you have developed, the beliefs you have created, the gratitude you feel, the contributions you make, all of which are positive and supportive and do take you in the direction of your goals?

• • • • • • • •

Keep this and refine, modify and add to it as you go through this program. This will become a great reference document for you.

AWARENESS EXERCISE SHEET #1B
Negative: What are the thoughts, beliefs, behaviors, disciplines that you have been consistently engaging in that are holding you back from achieving your goals?

You have 1 of 3 choices:

1. Burn this sheet of paper.

2. Tear it up into a thousand little pieces and throw it away.

3. Scrunch the page up into a ball and throw it away.

By doing this you are releasing the negative attitudes that you have recognized, not ignoring them, but choosing to no longer hold onto them. The exercise of "becoming aware" of these things helped you realize that these things are there. Holding onto them will only do harm and will not bring any good.

If you notice, as you are moving forward, that negative, poisonous thoughts and beliefs continue to rise, replace them with positive thoughts. We will reinforce the positive as we progress through this book.

Secret Number 2:
Set Your Intention from Your Desires

• • • • • • • •

Here's an excerpt from the classic book *The Man Who Tapped the Secrets of the Universe* by Glenn Clark, with a message that relates to our previous secret on awareness and ties in nicely with this second secret.

This book was written in 1946 and continues to be one of the most sought-after success books every written. The pages are filled with incredible, meaningful life messages, which you will glimpse in the next few short powerful paragraphs.

I believe sincerely that every man has consummate genius within him. Some appear to have it more than others only because they are AWARE of it more than others are, and the awareness or unawareness of it is what makes each one of them into masters or holds them down to mediocrity.

I believe that mediocrity is self-inflicted and that genius is self bestowed. Every successful man I have ever known, and I have known a great many, carries with him the key which unlocks that awareness and lets in the universal power that has made him into a master.

What is that key? I asked.

That key is desire when it is released into the great eternal Energy of the universe.

• • • • • • • •

Let's get right into the 2nd Secret to SMART Success, which is:

SET YOUR INTENTION FROM YOUR DESIRES

Setting your intention is deciding on an outcome in advance – simply put, making choices that will direct your future.

Setting your intention from desire will fuel the achievement of your goals.

Why is desire so important?
If you don't have a strong desire for a particular result, you will likely not stay focused on your goals. You will find obstacles and road-blocks to be increasingly more challenging. Or if you get knocked down, you may find it harder to get back up.

When you have a burning desire, you'll still experience obstacles and challenges, but the desire will be the boost that gets you back on track and pushes you forward.

If there were a straight and easy road to success we would all be on it. It would be crowded. But the way to success isn't crowded; the top isn't crowded. Why is that?

Because people aren't driven by their desires and don't set their intentions from their desires. They may also lack focus and are not aware. They are too easily thrown off course and do not engage the tenacity and the determination required. And the biggest barrier is the fact that they lack faith: faith in themselves, and faith in others.

All of these things are important:

drive   **awareness**
   focus   **faith**
              determination

• • • • • • • •

When you have the desire for the goal, you've got to follow through, and you will more likely follow through when you set your goals from your desires.

Choose Your Outcomes

In Secret Number 1 you were asked to decide on your desired outcome for *8 Proven Secrets to SMART Success*. When you did that, you set your intention based on a desire.

Why do this? Having the desire gives you the clarity to approach the book with an intended result, and thus you are likely to achieve that result.

You are already aware that you have the gift of choice. You choose how to respond to what shows up for you in your life, for instance. You choose what you will do with this valuable material that is now within your hands. And you can choose your intention.

As the saying goes:

"You are at choice always, in all ways."

Achieving goals is not an accidental occurrence. Achieving goals is the result of a pre-determined choice.

You see, you have unlimited opportunities and these opportunities are everywhere.

When you believe this, and know this to be true, new opportunities will be revealed to you. If you do not believe this, you will be blinded to new opportunities, even though they are likely directly in front of you.

● ● ● ● ● ● ● ●

Throughout my home I have a number of reminder statements. One of them, which relates to this secret, is:

If there is something you wish to experience in your life, do not "want" it, choose it.

In this chapter you will choose your outcomes by setting your intentions. But before we do, let's consider one of the reasons people never achieve their dreams.

Most people look at their own results for proof and validation of whether they can or cannot achieve a goal. When they can demonstrate that they were not able to create their opportunities in the past, or achieve their goals, they do not even bother to consider new possibilities.

People also look at other people's results and validate their own decisions by other people's negative results.

If you are looking for something, you will find it. If you are looking for an example to prove you can't do something, you'll get that answer. If you look for someone who has tried and failed, you will find the example.

On the other hand, if you open up your mind to new possibilities, and even though you may not have accomplished the goal in the past, you look for the example of someone who has accomplished incredible things, you will find it.

If you have an idea, then inherent within you is the ability to create it. You wouldn't have had the idea if you were not able to manifest it.

It is important to reject the belief that if something has not been done in the past it cannot be done in the future. If our inventors had believed that, we would not be able to communicate via cellular telephones, the Internet and computers. We would not be able to fly

● ● ● ● ● ● ● ●

across the country in a matter of a few hours, and we would certainly not be able to travel to the moon and return safely home.

Therefore, do not look at last year's results or any other previous result to determine your outcome as you move forward. Decide in advance where you would like to be. This will begin the creative process.

Do you know what you want in your life? Are you already fully aware of your dreams? Do you know for certain what you would have, do or be, if you could have, do or be anything?

Discover Your Passion
Before you set your intention it is important to know what you are passionate about. Do you know what you are truly passionate about? If you do, GREAT! Do this next exercise to confirm your passion. If you do not know what your passion is, pay particular attention to this next section.

Discovering what you are passionate about is simple to do. Simply think about what you love to do.

Think about what gives you the most pleasure.

How do you know you are passionate about something? Just recognize how you feel when you think of that thing. What do you talk about most of the time? What are you thinking about even when you shouldn't be thinking about it? Which book section do you go to at the bookstore or the library? Which magazines do you buy or look through? What subjects were most appealing to you when you were in school? What do you do research on? What are your hobbies? What are the things you really enjoy spending time doing?

Start to think about some of the things that you've done in the past that you became passionate about.

● ● ● ● ● ● ● ●

Think about a time in your life when you were the happiest and the most peaceful and remember what it was that you were doing, having or being.

Ask yourself the appropriate questions. You will get the answers. If you do not have answers to the questions immediately, ask again and again until you get the answers. Try doing different activities – drafting, gardening, public speaking, lecturing, a sales profession, writing – and use your gut instinct to determine your level of passion.

Here are the questions to help discover what you are passionate about. Record your answers as you ask the questions and review them later. Keep these questions for future reference.

Your passion may change as you get older, or your passion may change when circumstances in your life change, so you may want to keep these questions handy for future reference.

You can also use these questions to determine your continued level of passion after you have set your goals, to decide whether the goals you have set for yourself are true for you.

Here are the questions to determine your passion:

What do I really want to do with my life?
What am I passionate about?
What do I love?
Where would I go if I had the freedom to go anywhere?
What would I do if I could do anything?
What would I have if there were no limits?
Who would I become?
What gives me the most satisfaction in my life?
What do I really enjoy doing in my spare time?
What motivates me?
What inspires me?

• • • • • • • •

What excites me?

What drives me?

When I have had the experience of jumping out of bed with excitement, what was the cause?

What have I done in the past that has given me the most pleasure?

How do I want to contribute to the lives of others?

What would I like to give to others?

How would I like to be remembered?

If I were granted one wish, and I knew that that wish would be granted, what would I wish for?

You'll know what your true passion is by the way you feel when you answer these questions. When you reread your answer you will feel the blood rush in your veins. You will feel excitement and energy. You will feel inspired. You will want to get up and go!

Know your passion before you move on to the next part of this lesson.

Setting Your Goals

Are you a ship without a course? Have you decided clearly where you want to go with your life? If not, you need to get clear on what you would like to create in your life. Otherwise, you may float aimlessly around in an ocean of infinite opportunities.

When you choose to set your goals, you are setting the direction of your life. You are moving in a purposeful direction, with a clear understanding of the ultimate destination.

> **"I am the master of my fate; I am the captain of my soul."**
> – William E. Henley

Do you have your goals clearly written down?

Do you have goals for all areas of your life?

● ● ● ● ● ● ● ●

Do you feel inspired when you read them?

Most people do not set goals. Why? For many reasons:

- they don't know how to set goals
- they don't know how to achieve them and therefore do not bother setting goals
- they are not prepared to do the work
- they are afraid of what they'll have to sacrifice
- they don't believe in themselves
- they don't invest the time to really think about it

Now you will become increasingly more creative and play an active role in the creation of your goals as we get into one of the most important exercises you will ever do: Goal Setting.

> **"Cherish your visions and your dreams as they are the children of your soul, the blueprints of your ultimate accomplishments."**
> — Napoleon Hill

When we decide on a goal, it is usually not the goal that we want, but the feeling we'll get when we have achieved the goal. Ultimately, what goal setters truly strive for is a feeling, a state of being, such as happiness, peace, joy, ecstasy.

Goal setting involves making a decision about an outcome and writing it down; we could call this "a dream with a deadline."

• • • • • • • •

How Do I Know My Goal Will Be Achieved?

Desire is the starting point of all achievement. When you set a goal, you are planting a seed. When you provide the seed with the proper nutrition and attention, the seed will grow. Everything that is required to manifest your goals is available to you through the energy and the natural laws of the universe.

The ability to choose is one of our greatest gifts. We have the freedom to dream, to choose to have, be or do anything we desire. This is our birthright.

Inherent within everyone is the ability to achieve any dream we conceive. In order for the dream to become a reality, we must believe we can achieve it.

When you set a goal, your mind behaves like a missile. Once a missile is locked on a target, even if the target moves and changes direction rapidly, the missile will adjust to stay locked on the target. Similarly, when a plane is locked on autopilot, it will stay on course and automatically adjust if knocked off course.

When you set your mind on a goal, and keep your mind on the goal, even if you stray from your course, you will put yourself back on course and when you utilize your power of concentration.

So How Do I Set My Goals?

We will now look at the steps to goal setting.

* * * * * * *

STEP 1: Prepare yourself to set goals

To set your goals, start out with several blank sheets of paper, or a journal, and ensure that you have no distractions.

STEP 2: Choose Goal Categories

Before you start to write out the goals, choose the categories that you would like to have for your goals. Having the categories accomplishes two things: first, it encourages you to have balance in your life; second, it makes it easier to organize your goals.

The suggested goal categories are as follows:

- Career/Business
- Education
- Family
- Friends
- Finance/Savings/Income/Investments
- Home
- Personal Development (Health, Nutrition, Fitness, Skills)
- Travel
- Spiritual/Religion
- Contribution/Volunteer Work/Donations
- Things

STEP 3: Be in the highest state of being

Put yourself in a high-energy state of being, feeling great, excited and optimistic. You can achieve this high level of energy by playing your favorite upbeat music, breathing deeply, meditating, exercising briefly or whatever other activity puts you into a high state of energy.

● ● ● ● ● ● ● ● ●

STEP 4: Set the goals

This is the most important part of this exercise:

Write these goals as if you knew that you could not fail and your success was absolutely guaranteed. If you notice thoughts entering your mind like "how are you going to do that? or "you can't do that!" or any other negative thought, dismiss those thoughts and continue to dream big dreams. Use your imagination. Think of limitless opportunities and dream big.

Write out the goals as they come into your mind. Do not worry about the structure of the goal, or how you will achieve it, or the grammar; just write the goals as they come into your mind. Later in the exercise we will work on the goal statements and the steps for goal achievement.

Use these questions to initiate ideas or help stimulate your thought process as you go through this exercise.

What do you really want to accomplish?
- *get a degree: M.B.A., Ph.D., etc.*
- *achieve an award*
- *win a contest*
- *become a Vice-President within an organization*

Who do you really want to be (become)?
- *a well-known author*
- *a TV producer*
- *a philanthropist*
- *a successful business man/woman*
- *an executive*
- *a teacher*
- *a lawyer*
- *a medical doctor*
- *an outstanding parent*

● ● ● ● ● ● ● ●

What skills do you want to master?
- *the game of golf*
- *playing the piano*
- *being an outstanding hockey player*
- *a better time manager*
- *a great baseball player*
- *a great public speaker*
- *a gourmet cook*

What do you really want to have?
- *a new car: luxury, sports, 4-wheel drive*
- *a new home*
- *a new job*
- *your own business*
- *a boat*
- *new furniture*
- *a new wardrobe*
- *your own personal trainer*
- *a cook*
- *a 2-carat diamond ring*
- *a big-screen TV, DVD player and surround sound*
- *landscaped property, redecorated home*

What do you want to be recognized for?
- *your contribution to society*
- *your expertise in your field*
- *your work*
- *your ability to sing*
- *your talent on the piano*
- *being in outstanding shape*
- *your investment expertise*

How do you want your family/friends/partner/customers to feel about you?
- *you are a loving, caring and helpful friend*
- *you are generous to your family*
- *you are an extraordinary business person*

● ● ● ● ● ● ● ● ●

- *you are an honest and ethical individual*
- *you are an extraordinary parent/stepparent*

What would you do if you knew that you could not fail?
- *climb a mountain*
- *learn to fly airplanes*
- *travel the world and travel first class*
- *go on an African lion safari*
- *build a huge custom-designed home on a lake*
- *build a resource center for holistic healing*
- *be a multi-millionaire*
- *get married to the partner of your dreams*
- *improve the level of passion within your current relationship*
- *meet a celebrity, or someone you admire*
- *be in great shape physically and emotionally*

What are the targets you want to achieve (financially, in revenue, net worth)?
- *be financially independent by the time you are x years of age*
- *exceed last year's revenue by 100 percent*
- *increase your net worth by 25 percent each year*
- *donate a minimum of 10 percent of your income to the charity of your choice*
- *have at least $10,000 cash in your bank account at any time*
- *own your home outright*
- *pay cash for your brand new automobiles*
- *have all of the money to pay for your children's university education*

STEP 5: Review the list

Take the time to review your goal list. Keep a copy with you over the next week. Add to the list as ideas come to your mind. Goals can be added and removed from your list at any time. Do not be concerned with the number of goals that you have. There is no limit to the number of goals that you can have.

● ● ● ● ● ● ● ●

STEP 6: Select your top-priority goals

Once you have written out all of the ideas you can think of, go back through the initial goal list and select the top-priority goals from the categories. Again, the number of priority goals is up to you. There is no predetermined number that you need to select.

You can circle them to distinguish your top goals from the other goals.

STEP 7: Set the timeframe for achievement

Once you have selected the top-priority goals, you will now identify the timeframe for achievement. In other words, when would you like these goals to be realized? Some goals may be "ongoing" and you can label them as such.

Whether the timeframe is realistic is going to be based on beliefs. If you believe it is realistic, then it will likely be realistic. If you believe it is not, and continue to confirm that belief, you may experience greater challenges.

Set timeframes that cause you to stretch yourself beyond your normal comfort zones.

There are no hard and fast rules about what a goal is or is not. If there is something you want to have, do or be in your life, then it is a goal. Goals do not only refer to material items. Goals can also be characteristics or personality traits. If it is something you want that you do not presently have, then it is a goal.

A goal may also be something that you currently have and you want to continue to have; therefore, you have made it a goal because it is a priority. For example, if you currently have a very loving, passionate, honest, fun, caring, committed relationship with your life partner and it is something that is very important to you, then you may choose to have this as a written goal.

• • • • • • • •

Before we go on to the next step, let's talk about SMART goals. Some of you may be familiar with the acronym SMART as it relates to goals. I believe the **S** stands for Specific, the **M** for measurable, the **A** for achievable, the **R** for realistic and the **T** for time-sensitive.

For the sake of this book, I did not choose the word SMART for the goal-setting acronym. The reason I chose the word SMART is that you will enjoy success when you become aware of these proven secrets, engage your creative power, and implement these proven steps with unwavering courage, commitment and persistence.

And to elaborate, being successful is not only for people with higher IQ's. Success is something that you will achieve when you follow a few simple disciplines. It isn't rocket science; it isn't complicated: the simplicity of goal achieving is apparent from these 8 proven secrets (steps) to SMART Success.

STEP 8: Write out goal statements for your goals.

Goal statements are powerful statements. Repeating a goal statement over and over again, with conviction and sincerity, will start to build your belief systems.

Goal statements use the power of thought, one level of creative energy, and the power of word, another level of creative energy. When you consistently affirm a statement, it is only a matter of time before the energy of thought and word moves into form.

When writing your goal statements use the words "I am" or "I have" and do not use the words "I want." Why? Because "I am" and "I have" are declarations of your choice. The subconscious mind does not distinguish between what is real and what is vividly imagined. When you use the words "I want," the universe will respond and provide you with the experience of wanting the goal, not having the goal. Wanting something is always placing it in front of you and not claiming the goal as a choice.

● ● ● ● ● ● ● ●

The following are the guidelines to be followed when creating your goal statements. Ensure each and every goal statement follows these guidelines.

1. Write your goals in the present tense, as if you have already achieved the goal, using "I am" and "I have."

2. State your goals in the positive and choose your words carefully. For example, if your goal is weight-related, ensure that you write out your ideal weight and use words such as "slim," "ideal weight," "healthy," and do not use words such as "fat," "heavy" or "overweight."

3. Use "ing" verbs in your statement wherever you can (driving, enjoying, celebrating, flying, cruising, singing, etc.). For example; "I [your name] am proudly receiving the Award for . . . ." Verbs in the present tense will help you experience the feelings that you will have when you achieve this goal.

4. When writing out your goal statement, state your full name. For example, "I, Joe Smith, am gratefully enjoying being an example of outstanding contribution to . . . ."

5. Ensure the list of your top goals is written in your own handwriting, typewritten or computer-printed, and clearly displayed.

6. When writing out your goal statement be specific and clearly define your goal (if you are clear about the specific result you desire).

Goal Statement Examples
I, John Doe, am enjoying driving my brand new convertible BMW 535i.

I, Jane Smith, am enjoying being at my ideal weight of 115 lbs. I am fit and in excellent shape. I love to exercise and I do so on a regular basis.

• • • • • • • •

I, Bob Jones, am having a wonderful time on the Caribbean cruise with my new bride on our honeymoon. I have gratefully met and married the woman of my dreams. She is extraordinary and we love each other unconditionally. We treat each other with respect and honesty.

I, Mary Smith, am happily enjoying the beauty of the view from the window of our beautiful cottage on a clear and clean lake.

I, John Doe, am happily enjoying running my profitable and successful business. I offer tremendous value to my customers and as a result, they benefit from the use of our products. Our revenue this year has exceeded last year's numbers by 200 percent.

I, Bob Doe, am enjoying cutting our beautiful landscaped lawn with my brand new ride-on lawnmower.

I, Jane Smith, have gratefully paid for my home with cash. I now own my home outright. It feels great to know that I am absolutely financially free.

I, Brenda Jane, am enjoying the feeling of exhilaration after accomplishing my goal of earning my M.B.A.

STEP 9: Read your goal statements

Read your goal statements at least twice a day, every day. The best time to read your goals is just before you go to sleep. It is at this time that your conscious and subconscious mind are most receptive. This allows the subconscious mind to accept what you have written as a reality.

Take the opportunity to read your goals throughout the day. If you are sitting in traffic, take out your goals and read them. If you are waiting at the dentist's office, read your goals while you wait. If you are watching television, keep your goals handy, and read them during the commercials. Carry your goals with you wherever you go.

Share your goals only with people who will support you. If you think people will not support you and your goals, do not share your goals with them. This is important because it will allow you to avoid any negative input or possible non-empowering thoughts entering your mind.

If people will support you, share your goals. You may find these people to be great support and they may also intensify the energy.

When reading your goals say them out loud and say them with conviction. The intensity will contribute toward building the beliefs and putting energy in motion, as described earlier in the book.

• • •

So, if you could have anything, and I mean anything, what would that be?

- Dream big dreams

- Suspend any disbelief

- Imagine there are no limits

Be decisive and know your outcome!

"You will become as small as your controlling desire; as great as your dominant aspiration."

– James Allen

This chapter is not about the *how*. It is about deciding what you want.

And, until our next secret in *The 8 Proven Secrets to SMART Success*, remember this:

Life will show up for you no other way than the way in which you expect it.

Secret Number 3:
Take Consistent, Persistent, SMART Action

In Secret Number 2 you set clearly defined goals in all areas of your life.

But in order to realize your goals, you must take action.

Visualizing and writing out your dreams is not what it is all about in the real world. It isn't enough just to dream, or visualize; hard work is required. You cannot escape it; it's a must. It is essential to anyone's success.

So Secret Number 3 of *The 8 Proven Secrets to SMART Success* is:

TAKE CONSISTENT, PERSISTENT, SMART ACTION TOWARD THE ACHIEVEMENT OF YOUR GOALS!

In this section you will be given tools to take action to achieve your goals. These tools are easy to use and easy to apply to your life.

Taking action requires discipline to create new behaviors. As habitual creatures, we find it is easier to do nothing. And because we are habitual, we feel a natural tendency to go back to old habit patterns.

What you will learn in this chapter is how to create new habitual behaviors that will create a successful environment.

Follow these guiding principles, and you will meet with success.

"If one ADVANCES confidently in the direction of their goals, and endeavors to live the life that they have imagined, they WILL meet with success unexpected in common hours."
– Henry David Thoreau

He didn't say, "If one sits back and waits for the goals to show up. . . "; he said "if one advances," and that is precisely what we will do.

How Will We Advance?
When you set a goal, you have set the intention, and when you write down the goal as a clearly defined goal statement, the Law of Attraction is engaged.

Taking action helps this process along. Let me give you an example.

Imagine that your goal is a small pile of metal filings, and you are a magnet. Imagine the magnet is at one end of a long table and the metal filings are at the opposite end. The law of attraction is working – that is, the magnetic force is attempting to draw the metal filings to the magnet. However, because of the distance between the two, the desired result – connecting the metal filings to the magnet – is not going to occur. However, if you physically move the magnet toward the metal filings, as they are brought closer together the magnet force will connect the two.

The same principle works with achieving your goals. Taking action moves you closer to your goal.

"Faith without works is dead."
– The Bible

You can have the goal, you can think about it all of the time, you can read your goal statements, but if you don't DO anything about it, you will likely not achieve the goal.

• • • • • • • •

In order to develop new behavior patterns, you must begin and continue to do the things that create the new behaviors. In this case, I'm referring to goal-achieving action.

Tony Robbins talks about the overwhelming success that he realized at the beginning of his career. By the time he was in his late teens he was running a successful business and making more money in a month then most people were making in a year. He was nicknamed Wonder Boy. When Tony was asked what contributed to his success, he said that he took MASSIVE action toward his goals – not passive action, but MASSIVE action.

Taking action does not mean that you must take *massive* action. As long as you are taking some action toward your goal you will be moving in a forward motion and using the creative energy of action.

Once you set a goal, ask this question: "What will I do to take me in the direction of my goal and achieve the desired result?" WHAT WILL I is a pre-assumptive question: it assumes that you will do something, and this in turn causes you to take an action.

At first incorporating new disciplines into your life will feel foreign, especially if you start to do things that you normally did not do in the past. This creates a feeling of discomfort, but if you persist, the new behaviors will start to feel like normal everyday activities.

A friend of mine broke her right arm on the tailgate of the family station wagon when she was a young girl. Prior to the accident she was right-handed. Because her arm was placed in a cast and a sling, she was unable to use her right arm for several weeks. She had no choice but to use her left arm. By the time the cast was removed, she had become left-handed and to this day she remains left-handed.

● ● ● ● ● ● ● ●

At first, when you are adapting to new behaviors, it feels awkward and unnatural, just as it did for my friend when she first started writing with her left hand. But she persisted (at the time, of course, she had no choice if she wanted to be able to write).

So you must take action.

But What if I Don't Know What Action to Take?
Here's what I suggest:

- Find someone who can help.

- Create a mastermind alliance, a group of individuals who help support each other. Ask your mastermind members for suggestions.

- Search for the information. The Internet is jam-packed full of valuable and useful information.

Start by being clear about your goal, Then, look for the answers. Ask questions. You'll find them, if you look. Seek and ye shall find. Ask and the answers will be given to you.

Are you familiar with the dance called the Two-Step? Here is the Two-Step for this secret:

1. Make a plan and follow it.

2. Every day do something toward achieving your goal.

Creating a plan will take some time, but once you've done it, all you have to do is follow it and modify, if needed.

If you fail to plan, you plan to fail.

• • • • • • • •

I recommend that you make a plan by mapping out the outcome (the end result, the goal) and listing the activities that you need to do to achieve this outcome, along with the other critical success elements. And I have a phenomenal tool to help you do that:

GoalMAPS
Goal Management Achievement Planning System

GoalMAPS is a simple, easy-to-use planning tool for anyone who is committed to achieving their goals. GoalMAPS takes your goals and provides the vehicle for you to translate your goals into projects and activities, a little like a transparent road map.

Included in this chapter are the instructions for GoalMAPS, along with a blank template and a sample of a completed GoalMAP.

You can use the GoalMAP template for all of your goals, or only your top-priority goals (you decide how many you will list and how many you will work with at one time).

The GoalMAP template displays the goal, along with prioritization of the goals, target dates, metrics for achievement, status, activities, project plans and milestones. This is a real-time, dynamic, custom-designed goal achieving system. You can create this document in Excel or Word computer applications, to provide you with the flexibility to modify the columns and rows based on your own preferences (see sample later in this chapter).

On a regular basis, update the GoalMAPS report, and continue to update the report as needed. As you are progressing, you will be able to instantly notice which goals require attention.

What Are the Benefits?
- encourages your top-level performance
- increases focus because you are outcome-focused on goals
- helps you stay on course and puts you back on track if you get thrown off your path

● ● ● ● ● ● ● ●

- results-driven
- gives you the metrics to determine your measurement for success
- lets you assign priorities – you stay focused on the most important goals and activities

Here are your responsibilities when using GoalMAPS
- Define your goals.
- Find the resources to help you achieve your goals, and use them.
- Create project plans and activities, enter them in GoalMAPS, and incorporate them into your weekly agenda.
- Look for ways to over-achieve.
- Solicit help from others on how you can over-achieve.
- Measure your own success – continually.
- Notice what is working and what is not.
- Learn from mistakes or failures.
- If you are uncertain on how to do something, get some clarity.
- Create your mission statement and live your life On Purpose.

What Are the 10 Components of the GoalMAPS Report?
Here is a brief summary of the columns on the GoalMAPS report. There is a sample of a GoalMAP later in this chapter as a reference.

1. **Mission Statement** – (top of the report) This is where you enter your own personal mission statement, allowing you to stay on purpose. If you have a lengthy mission statement, summarize it into one empowering sentence and enter it onto the report.

2. **Name and Date** – Enter your name and the date of entry. When you update the report, change the date to reflect the most recent update.

3. **Goal Category** – Goal categories were defined in Secret 2. Please refer to that chapter and review the numerous recommended goal categories.

4. **Goal** – Write your goal statement here. Be certain that the goal is written as a goal statement following the goal statement guidelines in Secret 2.

5. **Complete Date** – The complete date is simply the date that you would like to have this goal achieved. If your goal is an "ongoing" goal – in other words, it is important to you all of the time, and you have decided that it will be an ongoing goal for you – then type the word "ongoing" in the Complete Date column.

6. **Priority** – It is recommended that you use a system of numbering for priorities. Therefore, 1 is highest (most important), 2 is medium priority and 3 is lowest. Or you may want to use words instead of numbers, and prioritize by "highest," "medium," or "low" priority.

7. **Status** – Create the words that have the most relevance to you. This column is designed to keep you focused on goals that require attention. This column will only have value when you use it, and I strongly recommend that you use this column for maximum benefit. Here are some suggestions for possible considerations for the Status column: "Over-achieved," "On Track," "Requires Attention," "In Serious Jeopardy." Or create a legend and color-code the cells to reflect the comments. For example, red could mean "in serious jeopardy," green could mean "on track," etc.

8. **Metric/Measurement** – This column is used for measuring your progress and/or determining the success factors that indicate achievement. If you have a financial goal, a number would be a measurement if the goal has no quantifiable measurement source, consider making a "feeling" a metric. For example, when

* * * * * * * *

you feel completely at peace, you have achieved the goal. You'll see samples of this in the sample GoalMAP that is included with this chapter.

9. **Resources** – In this column list the people who will help you achieve your goal and/or the resources that you will utilize (the books, courses, tools, information, research material, websites, etc.)

10. **Projects/Activities/Milestones** – This column is one of the most critical success factors for using a GoalMAP System. This is where you enter projects, activities and/or milestones related to your goal. A goal is just a dream, unless you take action toward the attainment of that goal. This column is where you will list the activities that you will do in order to achieve the goal. Ensure that you have activities entered for every single goal. This column is also the one that you will modify more than any other column. Keep this column up to date. You may also consider entering in the name of reports (business plans, marketing plans) that are more lengthy, detailed plans of execution.

How to use GoalMAPS

There are three easy steps to using GoalMAPS.

1. To start, enter all of the relevant information in each of the columns on GoalMAPS.

2. Update the Projects/Activities/Milestones column on a regular basis, as your activities change.

3. Change, modify or update the entire report as required.

    The output will only be determined by the input. As much as you put in, that is how much you'll get out. The better the planning, the better the result!

• • • • • • • •

GoalMAPS ⊕
Goal Management Achievement Planning System

Mission Statement:

Name:
Date:

Goal Category	Goal	Complete Date	Priority	Status	Metric	Resources	Projects/Activities/Milestones

● ● ● ● ● ● ● ●

GoalMAPS ✈

Mission Statement: To be the recognized regional leader in the field of physical therapy by providing the highest level of service and support to all of my satisfied customers.

Name: Mary Jane
Date: July 2002

Goal Category	Goal	Complete Date	Priority	Status	Metric	Resources	Projects/Activities/Milestones
Business	I, Mary Jane, gratefully have reached profitability in my business and I provide incredible value to my customers and a high level of income for me and my family.	Dec-02	1	on track	$100,000 per month in revenue	Marketing Consultant; Accountant; Business Plan	Implement our P.R. campaign; keep books up to date; introduce our referral program; measure and track performance, do at least 3 things each day to increase and improve business and service to our existing.
Health	I, Mary Jane, am happy being in excellent physical condition. I love to exercise and I do so on regularly. I eat foods and drink beverages that are healthy for my mind and body.	Sep-02	1	requires attention	eat well & exercise at least 3x/week	Personal Trainer; Healthy Living Books; Cookbooks; weights; gym	Run and workout at least 3 x a week in the morning, intensifying each workout; Read the healthy living book sitting on my dresser; Buy healthy foods from the local health food store, Cook healthy meals every day.
Family	I, Mary Jane, am enjoying investing quality time with family. My husband & I take time to be alone and invest quality time with our children.	on-going	1	requires attention	a happy family	Local Events Calendar; Bulletin Board; Church activities list	Review the local events calendar in our regional newspaper and engage the family in outdoor activities; play games with the kids, go cycling, swimming, roller-blading and soccer with the kids and my husband
Contribution	I, Mary Jane, am enjoying contributing my time to help support the National Cancer Society.	on-going	2	on track	Annual campaign; quarterly campaigns	Director for the Cancer Society	Help out with the neighbourhood campaign for the annual fund raiser; volunteer for the other activities to help organize fundraising events, Be the Team Leader and overachieve last year's fund raising event
Personal Development	I, Mary Jane, am enjoying having balance in my life and completely at peace and happy with who I am.	on-going	2	serious jeopardy	no stress in my body	massage therapist; books on getting and maintaining balance; relaxation tapes	Schedule a weekly 30 minute massage; listen to relaxation tapes early in the morning and just before bed and at 15 minute intervals throughout the day where required; study books on balance and implement the lessons learned.

THE **8** PROVEN SECRETS TO SMART SUCCESS

So the 3rd proven secret to SMART Success is to:

TAKE **CONSISTENT, PERSISTENT, SMART** ACTION TOWARD THE ACHIEVEMENT OF YOUR GOALS!

Being consistent means, *every day*, taking action toward the achievement of your goals. Build daily disciplines. Use a daily action planner, and schedule the activities.

Here are some examples of goal-achieving daily disciplines:

- read your goal statements the moment you wake up and just before going to bed, as a minimum, each day

- write down what you will do today to reach your goals (based on activities listed on your GoalMAP system)

- record the accomplishments each day

- plan your day, prioritize your activities, and follow your plan

At the conclusion of this chapter, you will also find a sample weekly planner. Whether you are using a manual diary, an electronic agenda or an application on a computer – whatever time management system you are using, you should be able to easily implement daily goal-oriented tasks into your plan.

Persistence means to never give up. In the great book *Think and Grow Rich*, author Napoleon Hill tells a story entitled "Three Feet from Gold," which illustrates the point that the most common cause of failure is the habit of quitting when one is overtaken by temporary defeat. This story is about Mr. Darby, a gold miner who sold everything he had to buy the proper equipment for gold mining, and mined and mined. Finally, after what seemed like a considerable investment of time and effort, he gave up his unsatisfying endeavor, sold everything to a junk yard, and moved away.

• • • • • • • •

The junk-yard man took a little time to plan, he did a bit of calculating, and then he called in an expert, a mining engineer. The expert said that the previous owner was not familiar with fault lines, and his calculations showed that the vein was just another 3 feet down from where Mr. Darby had stopped drilling. That is exactly where the gold was found.

Do you need to ask an expert? Maybe you are only 3 feet from gold and you simply need to call on someone who can help you.

If you are 3 feet from gold, keep going. Most people don't realize just how close they are, and they give up just before they are about to break through.

You may have heard that "it is darkest just before the dawn." Goal achieving can be like that too. It can seem bleak and unpromising, but if you give up, you'll miss out on the victory.

But How Will I Know?
Here's a paradox: it has been said many times, *Doing the same thing over and over again and expecting a different result is insanity.* This leads to the question: "When will I know if doing the same thing over and over again is insane, or if I'm simply 3 feet away from my goal?"

Well, sometimes you may not know. The recommendation that I can give you is to "go with your gut feeling." You are going to have to make the decision as to whether you keep going, or pack up and try another direction. Sometimes our gut instinct will be our guide; I have found in fact that when I trust my gut, I never go wrong.

Monthly Goal Achieving Activities
Earlier you were presented with daily goal-achieving activities. There are also a number of extremely effective monthly activities that will significantly contribute to the achievement of your goals. The following are proven, effective activities that will guarantee success when you consistently do them.

● ● ● ● ● ● ● ●

- Set monthly goals as stepping stones to reach your larger goals.

- Measure and monitor your progress.

- Measure and monitor your states of being (your feelings/emotions).

- Practice engaging in the states of being that support your goals (i.e., determined, focused, positive, grateful).

- Create a plan to achieve your goals and follow it.

- Create a contingency or backup plan.

- If your results are not the results that you desire, try something else.

- Enter action items into your daily schedule or time management system.

- Visualize yourself already in possession of your goals.

- Feel what it will feel like when you achieve your goals.

- Decide how you will celebrate when you achieve your goals.

- Establish your daily code of conduct (disciplines) and follow it.

- Stay focused on your goals in everything that you do.

- Ask yourself empowering questions.

- Keep an Accomplishment File and enter the goals once you achieve them. Add thank you cards and your favorite sayings. Review this file from time to time.

* * * * * * * *

- Be grateful for the gifts in your life and the gifts that you are creating.

- Acknowledge another for the gifts that they bring to your life.

"Progress always involves risk; you can't steal second base and keep your foot on first."
– Frederick Wilcox

Taking persistent, consistent SMART action is advancing your dream one step further. This means you are committed to that dream, for which you not only set the goal, but you are doing whatever it takes to achieve the goal . . . staying focused, overcoming challenges, creating and following a plan, and continually implementing methods of improvement.

Is Action Enough?
Being SMART is noticing what is working. Early in my career I had a job in sales. My sales manager used to scream at the sales team, "Sales calls, sales calls, sales calls."

Because the sales manager was looking for large numbers of sales calls, the sales team was not focused on quality calls or pre-qualified calls, but on numbers. So instead of doing 10 sales calls a week we would do 30. But did this help with the results? No. If anything, it made things worse. Here's why: the sales team became tired and discouraged, and many quit their jobs. We were not taught to schedule qualified and quality sales calls; we were taught that it is a "numbers game."

I can see the value in a numbers game. However, a SMART approach would be to schedule quality, pre-qualified calls; prepare for the call by establishing a desired outcome; set the expectations with the client prior to the appointment so that they know what to expect when you show up; and follow up after the call. That is a much SMARTER approach.

● ● ● ● ● ● ● ● ●

The message is that it isn't enough just to take any action; it is much more effective when you take SMART action – action that has been carefully planned and has a specific outcome.

Here is another tip for taking action:

If the goal seems too large, break down the goal into sub-goals.

If your goal is too big, and you don't believe you will achieve it, you may lose the drive or motivation to keep going. What I recommend is to break that goal down into smaller goals.

Let's use an example of a weight-related goal. I had a client who set a goal to lose 80 pounds. She had a hard time believing that she would achieve this goal; consequently, she would start to lose weight, and would get easily discouraged and go off track and gain the weight back.

I suggested that she make smaller, more realistic (from her point of view) goals – monthly goals, or even weekly goals – and start to work towards those. That is exactly what she did.

Here's what happened. When she reached the end of the first month, she found she had achieved the goal! Her determination intensified and her commitment became even stronger, because now she could see real results.

The next month, she exceeded her goal. On and on she went, until she lost 82 pounds. And, because she developed goal-achieving daily disciplines, she now maintains her new weight.

But here's the best news of all. Now that she has seen the power of goal achieving, she has applied it to her love life, and her finances, and she is now reaping the rewards of her commitment to achieving those goals.

* * * * * * * *

Remember that successful people are always taking action. Ponder, yes; plan, yes; and act, absolutely!

My friend Fernando Martinez has a Successories© Poster in his office that says:

> "SUCCESS: Some people dream about it, while others wake up and work hard at it."

We can summarize Secret Number 3 with a quote by Benjamin Franklin:

> "Humanity is divided into three classes: those who are immovable, those who are moveable and those who move!"

Be the one who moves.

WEEKLY PLANNER

Week of: _____

Goals Focused on This Week

#1 _____

#2 _____

#3 _____

#4 _____

Daily Goals Activity (What are my highest priorities for this day?)

MONDAY   TUESDAY

_____   _____

_____   _____

_____   _____

WEDNESDAY   THURSDAY

_____   _____

_____   _____

_____   _____

FRIDAY

_____

_____

_____

_____

SATURDAY

_____

_____

_____

_____

SUNDAY

_____

_____

_____

_____

_____

_____

_____

_____

Accomplishments

_____

_____

_____

_____

_____

_____

THE **8** PROVEN SECRETS TO SMART SUCCESS

Secret Number 4:
Believe in Yourself

This particular secret will transform your life, and every aspect of it, when you apply it.

What is the 4th proven secret to SMART Success?

BELIEVE IN YOURSELF

If you don't believe in yourself, you will struggle all the days of your life. And when you *do* believe in yourself, you will sail through your journey with ease and enjoyment.

Believing in yourself is having confidence, a strong sense of self-worth, high self-esteem and faith in *your* ability.

In this secret I'll share with you how to create the belief in yourself, how to change old beliefs into new, supportive, powerful, positive and empowering beliefs that will build a new wonderful vision of who you truly are – that beautiful, deserving and loving being.

Every one is born with confidence. Some exude it more than others.

Confidence is energy within you. Some have tapped into this energy, while others have not. But you all have it, whether you have tapped into it or not.

It's like the electrical power that is pumped into your home; the electricity is always there and there is an infinite supply, but it is invisible. If it's there, how do we use it? We access the energy by flipping a switch on the wall – a light switch.

Let's take that light switch one step further. Let's imagine that switch is a dimmer switch, or as my positive friends like to call it, "an illuminator switch," that will intensify or soften the light depending on whether you move the little control button on the switch up or down.

The more brightness you desire, the higher you move the control button. The limit to the brightness is the position where you choose to set the control.

If you place the control at the highest setting you will experience the greatest brightness.

Now let's take this analogy and apply it to confidence. Imagine for a moment that there are illuminator/dimmer switches within you. There are many switches, and these are energy switches to access states of being – emotional states and feelings.

On every switch there are two states of being: one extreme of an emotion and the other.

If we use the example of confidence, at the top of the switch is confidence and at the bottom is insecurity. You see, if you are not being confident, then you are being insecure. And this switch will move up or down depending on how you are feeling. The intensity of the emotion or state of being is determined by levels of energy.

Sometimes you may be extremely insecure and at other times you may be highly confident. You will experience confidence and insecurity for many areas of your life and at many different times. Your confidence switch keeps moving up and down at all times. It will

• • • • • • • •

move up or down depending on what you are doing, what you are thinking, and what you are saying (to yourself or to others).

Your beliefs help to determine where your switch is positioned. If you have a belief that you are an insecure person, even when you start to feel more confident, your beliefs will kick in and start to move your switch right back to the position that accords with your belief about who you are.

Each one of these states of being switches has two emotions. Every emotion has the opposing emotion at the other end. For example, if you take the love switch, at the top of this switch is love and at the bottom is hate. If peace is at the top of a switch, then stress is at the bottom. If happiness is at the top of a switch, then sadness is at the bottom . . . and so on.

Keep in mind that your emotional energy is available and will respond based on your desire. Moreover, you can decide how much of that energy you will use and when you will use it.

Your Creative Energy
Your thoughts are energy, your words are energy, and your actions are energy. This energy is either creative or destructive. Creative energy keeps your switches on high, or moves them up. Destructive energy moves those switches down, or keeps your switches on low.

I will show you how you can use all of your creative power to build a strong sense of self-worth and total belief in yourself.

Let's get into our first exercise.

If you were asked today, "how would you define yourself?" what would you say? Most people are shy about answering this question, because they don't want to admit (what they believe are) their faults, and they don't want to talk about their strengths, because they believe that is bragging.

• • • • • • • •

For the sake of this exercise, write out a clear description of who you believe you are. Be honest with yourself. Write out what you believe are all of your characteristics, your strengths, your challenges. Just list them on a sheet of paper . . . all of them. Include your positive qualities and your not-so-positive qualities.

Please put the book down now and make your list. Remember it is the *application* of wise thoughts that makes the difference.

When you are finished making your list, review the list and notice which beliefs are supportive and which beliefs are destructive.

My good friend William E. Bailey said, "How can you put on your make-up if you won't look at your face?"

You need to be willing to look at who you believe you are . . . today. Why? So that if you don't like what you see, you can change it. And, similarly, if you do like what you see, you can intensify those empowering qualities.

Everything that you have in your life right now – your finances, your relationships, your career, your health – has all been impacted by your belief of who you are.

Before we get into building a strong belief in you, let's look at the causes of low self-esteem, and how these things actually sabotage success. Here they are:

1. Looking at past results and determining the future accordingly

2. Having guilt for things done in the past and not allowing oneself to have any pleasure in the future because, at a deep level, one does not believe one deserves it

3. Blaming others, or blaming oneself, for past results

● ● ● ● ● ● ● ●

4.   Holding anger or resentment toward oneself or another

All of these negative emotions are anchors that will hold you back from success. An event does not determine who you are. You are not your past. It may have been who you were at the time, but it is not who you are truly.

Emotions such as guilt, unworthiness, blame, anger, resentment are strong negative emotions that must be released. If you are holding resentment and anger toward yourself or others, you have to move past that strong destructive emotion. These emotions are poison and they filtrate through your entire being, affect your self-esteem, extend out from you, go out into the universe and affect your results, *whether you are aware of it or not.*

At the time that Bob Proctor, my first mentor, came into my life, I had been doing two things. First, I was blaming everyone else for my unhappy life; second, I was angry with myself.

In my own case, I finally recognized the blocks and anchors that were keeping me imprisoned and holding me back. Once I became aware, I did something about it.

I've watched extremely skillful people fail miserably because they lacked confidence in themselves.

Notice the beliefs that you are holding onto that keep you stuck.

Have you ever uttered the words "that's just the way I am," and said it with defiance? I have. When people become defiant about who they are, and they are referring to a negative state of being such as impatience, stubbornness, anger, rudeness, disrespect, etc., trying to move them to a new belief is going to be a challenge.

● ● ● ● ● ● ● ●

So What Should I Do?

The first step is decision – a decision to look at the beliefs about who you are and analyze whether these beliefs are supportive or destructive.

Even if you have been labeled as a particular type of person, and it isn't a positive label, you can make those changes now.

Anther reason people stay as they are is that they know other people expect them to be that way. However, when you have decided on a new identity and start to be that person, even though at first your friends or colleagues will wonder why you are behaving in this new manner, after a while the labels will change and your friends and colleagues will see you as this new person.

At your essence, there is true greatness. It may be simply hidden, lying dormant and waiting for you to awaken it.

People love to be around confident people. Confidence will propel your career or business and allow you to enjoy fulfilling relationships.

> **"You become what you think about all day long."**
> – Ralph Waldo Emerson

And now, here are the most powerful keys to help you believe in yourself:

1. Think as a confident person. Notice your consistent thoughts. Are you thinking as a confident person? Think about what you are thinking about. Think about your greatest qualities, your positive strengths. Think about your greatest assets. Remember the accomplishments that you have had. Have only powerful, confident thoughts about yourself.

* * * * * * * *

"I think, therefore I am."
– French philosopher René Descartes

2. Be courageous. Successful people are not immune to fear; successful people take action in spite of fear. Move away from fear by acting courageously. When you are being courageous, you cannot be fearful. I'm not saying that fear will disappear, because the chances are it will not, but when you develop the state of being of courage, you'll be better equipped to move quickly from fear to courage, by first recognizing it, and secondly, taking action in spite of it.

3. Do good things for other people – unconditionally.
How can you "do good" for others?

- Buy your friend a beverage (smoothie, juice, coffee, herbal tea, etc.)

- Here's one that I've done that is fun to do: when you are in one of those drive-through line-ups, waiting in your car to buy a coffee, when you get to the pick-up window, pay for the coffee for the person in the car behind you. It will make them feel good – "wow, a complete stranger bought me a coffee today." And you, too, will feel good as a result.

- Buy the 2-dollar box of chocolates from the little boy who knocks on your door, who is out going door to door raising money for his hockey team.

- Make an unexpected telephone call to a friend, family member or loved one to let them know you care.

- Extend an invitation to a new friend to come to your home for afternoon tea, dinner, brunch or just coffee.

- Send a card with kind words for no particular reason.

* * * * * * *

- Leave a rose on a friend's car or desk with a note saying, "Someone cares about you."

- Smile at a stranger.

- Open a door for a stranger.

- Give a portion of your income away. It's called tithing. It doesn't have to be a large amount or an actual tenth of your income (the original meaning of "tithing"); do it when you feel like it. Sometimes you may give more than other times. Choose the recipients (charities, organizations, church) that are most important to you.

4. Be kind to EVERYONE. Even if you think that someone doesn't deserve it.

This may be a challenge when someone appears to be undeserving, but consider this statement: People need love and understanding the most when they deserve it the least.

Use your manners and treat people with respect, kindness, thoughtfulness, warmth and friendliness. And when someone is speaking with you, look them in the eyes and give them your undivided attention.

5. Show your appreciation to others. Quite often we take others for granted; we may feel appreciation, and forget to mention it. Take a moment to say "thank you" or "I appreciate you" and do this often. Everyone wants to feel appreciated.

6. Become a great communicator. Learn to become a polished public speaker. Join the Toastmasters organization and become a great communicator. Even if your life does not require you to be a public speaker, this one quality alone will help you increase your self-esteem considerably.

7. Be a solution provider – to your own life's challenges and to others'. Look for the solutions to every challenge. Help others find the solutions to their challenges. Become known as a "solution provider." If you experience a challenge with finding an answer, persistently look for ways that it can be done, not ways that it cannot.

8. Compliment others often and do it with sincerity. Get into the habit of complimenting people often. Compliment strangers. Let them know if you like their suit, or their hair style, or the color of their eyes. Or if you see a parent being extremely kind and patient to their child, let them know that you noticed.

9. Humbly, accept compliments when they are given to you. This is one of the hardest things for insecure people to do – accept a compliment. Simply say "thank you" when you receive a compliment. Or you may accept a compliment and extend one at the same time by saying something like "thank you; you are so kind for saying that."

10. Stay positive in spite of the negativity around you. Negativity is everywhere. It can be extremely hard to avoid, but when you hear it, let it bounce off of you. Do not engage in conversations that are complaining or gossiping. If someone is being critical to you, or gossiping about another, that's negative, and you need to imagine a transparent shield around your body that repels negativity. You are at choice as to whether you let the negativity in or not.

Never, ever, ever be disrespectful by speaking negatively to yourself about yourself . . . whether you are joking or not. I was at my friend's home once and she said out loud, "How can I be so stupid!" I immediately piped up and said, "Please do not speak like that about yourself. That is self-destructive. Quite possibly you simply made an error in judgment, that's all. Do not make it more than it is."

● ● ● ● ● ● ● ●

Hang out with positive people. Keep positive motivational audio programs close at hand and play them for positive reinforcement. Use positive affirmations, place reminder cards around your home or your work place with your favorite positive quotes. Read positive books. Watch positive movies. Read magazines that are filled with great success and motivating stories.

11. Take care of your physical body. The way you eat, the beverages that you drink, and the exercise that you do (or don't do) all affect the way you feel about yourself. Eat and drink only those foods and beverages that are good for you. Learn about nutrition and apply it in your life. Drink plenty of water, rest when you need to, and exercise your physical body on a regular basis.

Another part of taking care of your physical body is personal hygiene. Take care of yourself with personal grooming, and dress for success. Build the wardrobe of a successful person. You have only one opportunity to make a first impression. Whether you like it or not, people will decide who you are based on your physical appearance.

Taking care of yourself also involves your posture and body movements. Move as a successful person. Stand tall. Allow the confidence to come through your physical body. When a person is confident you can see it. They walk as if they are confident, they perform with confidence, and their results are superior because of their level of confidence.

And enjoy simple indulgences. Treat yourself kindly. Buy yourself a new outfit. If you are a woman, get your hair and your nails done. Order the Café Mocha instead of the regular coffee. Buy the raspberries even when they're not in season and are ridiculously expensive – because you deserve it.

* * * * * * * *

12. Develop and use positive language through your speech and vocabulary.

When asked the question "How are you?," respond with "Wonderful! Fantastic!" Say it with enthusiasm. Say it with confidence. When I ask someone how they are, quite often I hear people say, "not that bad." And I'll respond with, "It's bad, just not *that* bad?" Be cautious of the words that you are using. Remember WORD is an energy that is working toward creating your results.

The other day I was at the clubhouse and I met up with a fellow golfer, just as we were about to tee off. I asked him, "How are you feeling today?" He responded with: "If I had a tail, I'd wag it." This fellow golfer is an enthusiastic and positive communicator.

Eliminate the word "impossible" from your vocabulary. Eliminate any and all negative language. If you let negativity come into your life, it will, like a demolition ball, destroy everything you are building in one fell swoop.

Use positive words to encourage others. Help build another person's self-esteem by saying things like "You can do it! I know you can. Believe in yourself. You've got everything you need to make this happen. Everything you need is within you now. Make it happen. You have the power and the ability."

When you leave a conversation, always leave on a positive note. Leave the person feeling energized, smiling, or feeling they are special and cared about.

13. Go the extra mile.
Take the opportunity to do more than you are asked, required, or expected to do. You can do this everywhere, in business and in your personal life. When you are visiting friends, help out with meal preparation and/or clean-up. At work, do more than is expected. If an employer has an expectation for your role, be clear on what they expect, and exceed it. Your customers will

certainly have expectations. Build your business with the philosophy of giving them more than they bargained for.

And if you are asked to go the extra mile . . . do it. Not with resentment, or any other negative emotion, but with pride and gratitude.

14. Add value to other people's lives. Think about ways and means by which you can add value to another person's life.

Ask yourself these questions:

- What can I do to help them?
- How can I assist another to be more effective or successful?
- What will I do to add more value in this situation?
- How will I benefit others?

15. Be grateful. How will gratitude increase your level of confidence? Gratitude helps you focus on the positive aspects of your life. Be grateful for *your* gifts. Be grateful for who you are. Be grateful for your intellect, your physical abilities, and the opportunities you have and have created for yourself. Be grateful for the gifts you bring to other people's lives.

16. When you make a commitment, follow through. Stand by your word. If you find that you cannot follow through, and you have made a commitment, let the person know. Do not leave people waiting or hanging on. When you make a commitment people set up an expectation, and they are now counting on you. When you follow through you are actually building your confidence. Not following through will hurt your confidence. So when you give someone your word, do what you say.

17a. Make a decision when a decision needs to be made.

• • • • • • • •

17b. Stick to your decision once you have made it. Being decisive confirms a confidence within. Sticking with your decisions confirms the confidence to an even greater extent.

18. Be honest with yourself and with others. Always tell the truth. Withholding the truth is dishonesty. Honesty is the highest form of love. Speak the truth and the truth shall set you free.

19. Be an observer and not a person who is judgmental. Being judgmental lowers self-esteem. Observation gives you choices.

When you say the words "that's awful," that is judgment. If you say "that's interesting," that is an observation. Observation implies that it is neither good nor bad. Noticing without judgment is observing.

If someone cuts you off on the highway, rather than saying "oooh, that so-and-so," say "I wonder what caused this person to drive in this manner." This is an observation. You are not experiencing any negative emotions. Frankly, even if you did experience a negative emotion, the other person is long gone and has no idea that they have affected you. Do not allow this to ruin your day. Move past it with an observing attitude.

Make observations that allow you to make new decisions. Observing will not cause you to feel bad and it will move you forward.

Make a conscious decision to no longer be judgmental of others or of yourself.

Be an observer of your strengths and abilities. This involves heightening your awareness and observing your own positive character traits. Interestingly enough, most people will often grossly overestimate the ability of another and grossly underestimate their own ability.

• • • • • • • •

20. Take what you believe are your "downfalls" – the negatives – and see them as strengths, as positive.

You can do one of two things with what is commonly known as negative traits. One, change them to the positive (move them up the scale to the opposite end of the emotion, and thus turn a stressed emotion into a relaxed state of being).

Two, see the positive side of this character trait. Let me give you some examples:

If you believe that you are highly emotional: turn that into a positive and see yourself as being caring and sensitive. This is a subtle difference with a positive effect.

If you are impatient: you can look at this as having a strong desire to get results and could quite possibly be called determined.

If you are too honest: you can never be TOO honest. Honesty is an admirable quality and in this particular case, all you have to do is look at it as a positive quality and ensure you are communicating your honesty in a loving and respectful manner.

If you think you are a perfectionist: depending on how you make this statement – in a positive tone or a negative tone – being a perfectionist could also mean that you do everything with careful consideration and do your best. This too can easily be turned into a positive.

If you consider you are an over-analyzer, you may choose to look at this characteristic as making cautious, carefully evaluated decisions, and not careless decisions.

A person who is unfocused may be considered to be a free spirit and someone who doesn't get caught up in increased tension.

* * * * * * * *

If you are the type of person who views yourself with a critical eye, take a new look and view yourself in a new light, a positive light, and see the advantages to the personality traits that you do have.

Here's a caveat. If you are engaging in harmful, negative states of being then I do not suggest you try to look for the good in that. I suggest you eliminate or replace these harmful behaviors. If you do have destructive behavior that is causing you pain, or causing any one else pain, then I highly recommend that you replace those negative states of being with positive states of being.

Finally, in summary . . .

Be the person that you dream of being. Who you are is a process of creation. Be who you wish you were!

Start by falling in love with yourself. The first love is self-love.

Build an identity for yourself that matches your goals. Take a look at your goals and answer this question: "Who do I need to BE, in order to HAVE this?"

How Can I Bring All These Together?

Read all of your goals, and once you have gone through the entire list, write out an empowering, moving, motivating, inspiring identity statement of who you are. Your identity statement can be a combination of positive affirmation statements.

Here's a sample of the identity statement of one of my clients:

I display and express gratitude, appreciation and thankfulness for all of the wonderful gifts in my life.

I am successful beyond my wildest dreams in all areas of my life and a true example of possibility. My life is an inspiration to others.

● ● ● ● ● ● ● ●

I love unconditionally. I am loving, determined, driven, persistent, committed, courageous, kind, confident, thoughtful, caring, warm, friendly, enthusiastic, patient, fun, resourceful, spiritual, creative, genuine, wealthy, understanding, trustworthy, generous, professional, classy, talented, brilliant, wise, healthy, sporty, toned, energetic, passionate, honest, organized, efficient, peaceful, calm and focused.

I have complete faith in God and I have complete faith in myself.

I am an outstanding, loving, nurturing, patient, kind, thoughtful, fun parent. I am a wonderful, loving, giving, committed, gentle, considerate Life Partner. I am in great shape and I take great care of myself.

My income and my net worth are constantly increasing. I am classy and dressed impeccably at all times. I conduct myself in a professional manner at all times. I am abundantly wealthy. I have an excellent understanding of effective investment strategies and I utilize them to constantly increase my investment portfolio and reap the financial benefits. I am committed to helping others by generously giving financial contributions and time contributions. When I make a commitment, I follow through.

I am significantly and positively making a contribution in the lives of others.

Create your identity statement and read it every single day: in the morning and just before retiring at night. When you are reading it, read it aloud and with conviction.

Practice all of these things and you will develop an unwavering belief in yourself.

Confidence is an inside job.

• • • • • • •

You will not get confidence from something outside of yourself. If you seek to gain confidence from a job or a relationship or from some other source, you are setting yourself up for disappointment.

I've seen extremely talented people become insecure when they lost their job, because they had tied their confidence level to their career. I've seen athletes leave their profession as athletes and become bums in the street because they had all of their confidence tied up in their athletic ability and their athletic performance.

Believe in yourself. Have faith in your abilities regardless of what it is that you are doing. Remember, confidence comes from what you are BEING.

Whenever you feel yourself getting off track, ask yourself this question: "Is this who I am?" This is one of the most powerful questions that you will ever ask.

You've been given one of the greatest secrets to success. Practice these steps. There is a wonderful person waiting for you to discover. All you have to do is look in the mirror and you will see that perfect being staring back at you.

Secret Number 5:
Have Absolute Faith

● ● ● ● ● ● ● ●

> "To believe in the things that you can see and touch is no belief at all, but to believe in the unseen is a triumph and a blessing."
>
> —Abraham Lincoln

You need to really think about that statement for a moment.

Dr. Wayne Dyer has a marvelous program and book called: You'll See It When You Believe It.

Most people think this statement should be the other way around: "I'll believe it when I see it."

I'm here to tell you that Wayne has the order of that statement perfect! You will see your goals when you believe that you'll see them.

The 5th secret to SMART Success is

SEE YOUR GOALS IN ADVANCE AND HAVE ABSOLUTE FAITH OF THE ACHIEVEMENT

In addition to having the faith in yourself that we talked about in Secret 4, you will also require a deeper belief and a faith in possibilities; a faith in the Universe, faith in God and faith in others.

● ● ● ● ● ● ●

You have the power within you to achieve any goal. This power is superior to any condition and any circumstance.

As it has been said repeatedly, "We can alter our lives by altering our states of being." Absolute faith IS a powerful state of being. It is a state of being just like the other states of being that I've talked about in this book: confidence, love, success, fulfillment, happiness, joy, peace, etc.

People with faith are more relaxed because they are not anxious. They know the perfect result will occur. When you have faith you'll keep your finger off the panic button. If you have absolute faith, you are not anxious, doubtful, stressed, or worried. You know the perfect result will occur; therefore, there is no reason for these self-destructive emotions (stress, doubt, insecurity, etc).

When you have absolute faith, doubt is absent. If, however, doubt creeps in, be aware. Determine at what level you are entertaining doubt and how often.

If your faith is not strong, doubt will break through. Imagine doubt as a thin bubble around you and negativity is a stick pin: when the stick pin hits the bubble it will pop it. On the other hand, if you have absolute certainty, you have surrounded yourself with a strong Plexiglas bullet-proof shield and negativity will not get through.

You are a co-creator working with an infinite power; the potential is unlimited. What is true of the great achievers in our history is true for us. Have faith that you too have infinite possibilities to create extraordinary things.

Faith has a mystical quality, and creates what we call "coincidences" or "luck."

● ● ● ● ● ● ● ●

A number of years ago I decided that I would buy a home for my son Michel and me. I had only one problem – I didn't have any money. And, apparently, you need some of that when you are going to buy a home, especially when the one that I chose was listed for a quarter of a million dollars. I clung to the image of Michel and me living in our home, created a feeling of faith that we would have it, and within a six-month period of time I made all of the money I needed to buy our brand new, professionally decorated, 4-bedroom home in a beautiful neighborhood.

Henry Ford had a belief that he could make an 8-cylinder motor, and even though he was told by his employees that it couldn't be done, he insisted they do it. He had faith that it could be done, and they did it!

President Kennedy had faith that we could put a man on the moon in a decade. The people did not believe him. Walking on the moon had never been done before. However, within a 10-year period Neil Armstrong had taken one small step for man and one giant leap for mankind.

There are 3 levels of faith around everything.

The first level is hope. You are hoping for something. You are wishing that it come true, or that it will happen. But you have NO certainty. However, please know that there is a certain amount of creative power in hope. It may not be as powerful as absolute faith, but there still is creativity, at a low level.

The second level is belief. At the level of belief you think something is true, or that it will happen, but you are still not quite certain. There is still an element of doubt when you are in this stage. You are easily pushed back to hope, and feel stressed when obstacles are put in your way.

And then there is the state of absolute faith, where you are completely certain. There is no doubt. You are as certain of the outcome as you are that the sun will rise and set tomorrow.

When you are in this state of absolute faith you expect challenges. You know that obstacles are a part of the natural occurrences and you easily move through them.

When you have absolute faith, you do not allow anything to take you off track. You don't consider an obstacle a distraction or even a nuisance; you simply see it as part of the perfection of everything. In the face of adversity, you hold strong to your faith and are unmoved and unaffected as a result.

When you feel this absolute faith you are consciously aware of the state of being that you are in.

Faith is beyond belief. Faith is an absolute certainty, a knowing of an outcome. When you have faith you have no doubt that the result will be obtained.

Quite often you'll see people move from one stage to another. From hope to belief to faith, and sometimes right back to hope. What you need to learn is to move to the state of being of absolute faith and stay there.

My question to you is: "What do you choose?" Do you choose to stay between hope and belief, or even stay in doubt? Or will you choose absolute faith?

Quite often people will ask me, "why would I choose to stay in doubt?" Simply, it is because it serves you somehow to stay in that state of being. How does staying doubtful serve someone? Staying in a place of doubt keeps you in your comfort zone. You can also justify not doing anything if you don't believe it can be done.

In Christopher Reeve's marvelous new book, *Nothing Is Impossible*, he says, "The vast majority of people live within a comfort zone that is relatively small. The comfort zone is defined by fear and our perception of our limitations. We are occasionally willing to take small steps outside it, but few of us dare to expand it."

Being in doubt allows you to justify your own actions, or lack thereof.

Think about one of your goals for a moment. Think of something that you have wanted for a long period of time and answer this question:

What is my level of faith with regard seeing this goal achieved? Do I believe with absolute certainty that I will achieve this goal or have I entertained doubt?

The answer to this question will determine your level of faith.

As soon as you set a goal, you've set the intention. You've started to create that reality. The moment you start to entertain doubt, you start to create *that* reality (not achieving the goal). Having belief or faith, and then moving to doubt, is like going forward and then moving backward. Therefore, have faith and you will move forward. Consequently, have doubt and you will move backward.

having faith = moving forward
having doubt = moving backward

That's it — see the power, see the effect.

Some people experience a "defining moment": a moment when they simply say, "that's it, I'm doing it and nothing is going to stop me." At that precise moment they've moved into a decision that creates a certainty. It is almost as if the two move together: the decision to do it, and the certainty that it will be done.

* * * * * * *

How Can I Experience Certainty?

Since being absolutely certain isn't always that easy for everyone, there are things that you can do to help you get there. The question I hear more often than any other is this: "How can I BE absolutely certain?" "What are the things that I can do that will help me be certain?"

Here are some very powerful methods to help build your faith in your achieving of your goals:

1. Visualize yourself already in possession of your goal.

2. Act as if you have already achieved your goal.

3. Write out your top goal on a 3" x 5" goal card and carry it with you wherever you go and read it.

4. Write out a detailed description of your life as you would like it to be. This is called *scripting*.

1. Visualization is seeing all aspects of your life as it will be, in advance of achieving your goals.

When you see yourself already in possession of your goal, and you do this often, you create an image in your subconscious mind and you actually feel the feelings in your body. Your subconscious doesn't know if it is real, or not. And if you continue to see yourself with it, the natural laws will work with you to create the manifestation of your visualization.

2. Act as if you are successful and you will become successful. Have faith that what you want to come to you will come to you, and you don't have to know how it will happen. I want to restate the last part of that last sentence: you do not have to know how it will happen.

• • • • • • • •

THE **8** PROVEN SECRETS TO SMART SUCCESS

As soon as you think of a goal, the natural instinct is to say, "How will I do that?" If you decide that you need to know "how" you will likely get immediately thrown off course. If you knew how you would have done it by now. And if you keep going to this place in your mind, trying to answer "How am I going to do that?" you stop the flow and cut yourself off from the possibility because you don't have the answer . . . at that moment. You have to have faith that it will come and hold on to that faith. It may come from "left field," from some place that you are not expecting, but it will come nonetheless when you have absolute faith.

3. Write out the goal statement for your top goal on a 3-inch by 5-inch index card and carry it with you everywhere you go. Pull out your goal card and read it often. Make sure that when you read your goal card you feel yourself already in possession of this goal. Get emotionally involved in the experience as you read the card.

4. Write out a description of what your life is like now that you have achieved all of your goals. This exercise is called scripting. You write out a script for your life as if you were a screenplay writer writing a play. When this screenplay is played out you get emotionally involved in the script because of the details and intricacies of the imagery.

Being Certain
Let's go back to the question asked earlier in this secret: "What are the things that I can do that will help me to be certain?" If I were to dissect that last sentence, what we would actually find is that the sentence is backwards.

First BE certain, and then do the things that a person with certainty would do!

● ● ● ● ● ● ● ●

Are you aware that there is a hunger problem in this world? I'm certain that you are, but did you know that there is an even greater hunger than food, and that is the hunger for faith? People want to have faith, but they don't have it. Here's the irony, there is no shortage of faith. Faith is omnipresent. If you want it, you can have it. You can turn it on, or turn it off. You can intensify it, or you can weaken it.

Consider this for a moment: when you are in love you don't decide, I'm going to fall in love, you just do. The love is within you. It wasn't something that someone injected into your bloodstream; it wasn't something you drank; you already had it within you. Love is a state of being that is within each of us. Just like faith. Faith is within you and you only need to recognize it, and bring it forth.

Just Do It
Here's how to build faith. Act as if you are now living the life that you have set as your intention from the goal-setting exercise. Imagine what your life will be like once you have achieved all of your goals.

Dive deep into your imagination for a few minutes and let's visualize. Do it . . . prepare yourself to expand your imagination.

Start to think about your goals, the dreams you have, the desires you have, things you wish for, long for, and deeply want to have, do or be in your life. Think about what they are and then start to feel what it feels like to achieve them.

Visualize as you do this, and in your body imagine what it feels like now that you having everything that you ever dreamed of. Your life is complete.

Experience the sense of accomplishment that you feel now that you have achieved your goals. Say the word "Wow!!!" out loud and feel the exhilaration of knowing you have arrived. You've done it; you've accomplished your goals.

● ● ● ● ● ● ● ●

Feel the gratitude that is sweeping over your entire being for all the gifts in your life.

Keep visualizing and get the visuals of you with everything that you desire for yourself. Create the vivid picture of you living your life as you now choose to live your life.

See every aspect of your new life and see it vividly, look at the details, see the home that you live in . . . walk in the door of your home, look around; what do you see? Who do you see? What do you feel? Can you feel the love . . . can you feel the joy . . . can you feel the warmth of your home? Go through all of the rooms of your home . . . look at everything inside . . . see the quality furniture, stop and look at the photographs on the mantel, feel the quality of the flooring you are walking on, see the perfection of the design. Is there a fire burning in the fireplace? Are the windows large and giving you a beautiful view of the magnificent, landscaped gardens? Step through every room and see them as clearly as if you are walking there right now.

Who is in your home with you? Who do you enjoy this gorgeous environment with? Who do you love? Who loves you? How much fun are you having together, as a family? Feel the sense of knowing that you are with your loving and close family and the love is expressed unconditionally, easily and effortlessly.

Now step outside and get into that brand new automobile. Smell that scent of a new vehicle. Feel the leather of the steering wheel. Turn the key in the ignition and hear the sound of the motor. Feel the sense of gratitude for driving such a fine piece of machinery. Drive down the road, and feel the amazingly smooth ride . . . really enjoy every aspect of this drive . . . the scenery, the ride, the incredible sound of the finest stereo as it is pumping out your favorite music.

● ● ● ● ● ● ● ●

And now look at your fulfilling career or business . . . . What are you doing? See yourself enjoying it immensely. You are totally successful in business. Success has become a way of life for you. You make it look easy.

See your healthy, toned, fit and energy-filled body. Feel the energy that you have being in top physical condition. See yourself loving the exercise program that you are diligently involved in. You love to exercise and do so on a regular basis. If you miss a day, you can't wait to get back at it. And, taste the mouth-watering healthy and nutritious foods that you are blessed to eat each and every day. All of your nutrition needs are met before you even ask.

Your life is complete. You travel with style to the most elegant and luxurious destinations. Your family travels with you and you have the most magical and memorable times of your life.

Your needs are met even before you ask. You are blessed, you feel blessed, and you give thanks. You give so much of yourself to others . . . with large financial donations supporting your favorite charities, volunteering your time and making contributions with your skills and vast knowledge.

You see yourself having celebratory dinners with your friends. Look around the table and see the faces of the many friends who love you and whom you love. See the smiles and hear the laughter as you enjoy these magical evenings.

You create memories that last a lifetime and you cherish them.

You are abundantly wealth in every sense of the word. You are healthy, wise and fun. You and your family are enjoying a lifestyle of opulence and luxury!

● ● ● ● ● ● ● ●

See every aspect of you life as you want it to be . . . see every detail . . . see the clothes you are wearing . . . smell the flowers in your garden, taste the fresh fruit from your trees . . . breathe in the clean fresh air as you are standing tall . . .

See the smiles on the faces of those that you love. Listen to the laughter in their voices. Hear the joy and elation they are experiencing because you are giving unconditionally.

Feel the sense of peace that you have knowing that you are now living your life on purpose and you are living your life based on your highest values.

People look up to you, you're a leader . . . you are a true achiever and everyone knows it.

You now know that you can do anything you set your mind to. You believe in yourself. Your family and friends believe in you. You are a winner. People love to be around you. People find joy being in your presence.

Now I want you to feel that faith even stronger . . .
And feel that state of Absolute certainty,
Where you know that there is no question in your mind that you have achieved everything you want.

Feel the certainty right now.
Expect it to happen.
There is no question in your mind WHATSOEVER!
Stand up and feel that certainty right now!
You are a goal achiever.
You expect it.
And you know its achievement is certain.
Take a deep breath in and feel that feeling of absolutely certainty.
Smile because you have that faith.
Now you expect success, you know it, and you're excited about it.

● ● ● ● ● ● ● ●

What are you seeing in your mind? What are you picturing now that is different from before?
Feel that certainty.
Feel it in your body.

Your certainty is stronger than no other.
You have an absolute feeling of knowing.

You truly are the best.
You are unstoppable . . .
You are unbeatable . . .
There is boldness, genius and infinite power within you.
You know with your entire being that you are a true achiever!
Feel it in your body.
Feel it.
You've got it . . . absolute certainty.

Your friends are proud of you!
You've got it.
You are outstanding and nothing's going to stop you.
The whole world knows you're an achiever and you know it too.

Right now, today, at this very moment, you know that nothing can stand in your way. When you need extra determination, you've got it. When you need more energy and drive, you've got it. You've got all you need inside you now!

Today is one of those days when nothing can stand in your way. You are incredible, and today is the day that you are strong, confident and more determined than ever! You believe in the impossible. You turn the impossible into the possible.

You are creating an extraordinary destiny!
You have absolute certainty and you feel it in every ounce of your body, and now the world will see it in your results!

* * * * * * * *

Now, how did that feel? Do it again. Visualize as you do it. Intensify the experiences each time you do this exercise.

Do this exercise often. Train your body to believe, to have faith. It is a full-being exercise that needs to be done over and over again to reinforce your belief system.

When you are walking down the road walk as if you have absolute certainty, breathe as if you have absolute certainty, and talk as if you have absolute certainty.

> ### "Act as if it is impossible to fail."
> – Dorthea Brand

I guarantee you, it will only be a matter of time until you are so certain that you don't even have to think about it any more.

Earlier in this chapter I said that you don't have to know how you are going to achieve your goal. With faith, the how will show up. You will attract the how to you, and when you least expect it, there it is!

Be the successful person who always sees the end result before anyone else.

> ### "Anything the mind can conceive and believe it will achieve."
> – Napoleon Hill

You might have to read this 5, 10, or maybe 50 times. Even if you have it in your consciousness, in your intellect, this does not mean that you have it in your being.

Read it often, and begin by knowing that you have already arrived.

● ● ● ● ● ● ● ●

Secret Number 6:
Overcome Obstacles, Adversity and Challenges

• • • • • ● • •

"It's the constant and determined effort that breaks down all
resistance, sweeps away all obstacles."
– Claude M. Bristol, author of *The Magic of Believing*

What is the 4th proven secret to SMART Success?

OVERCOME ALL OBSTACLES, ALL ADVERSITY AND EVERY CHALLENGE

Find anyone who has achieved success and you'll find an individual
who has had to overcome obstacles, endure adversity and work
through challenges.

Challenges are universal and they are constant. There is no way to
escape them. There isn't an individual or an industry that isn't
experiencing or won't experience challenges.

At some point in your life you will be faced with adversity. Lou
Holtz, the famous football coach, once said "If adversity isn't
hitting you right now, it's coming. So get ready for it."

• • • • ● • •

Some people look at successful people and say "they are so lucky" and think that they don't have any challenges. Well, I'm here to tell you that isn't the case. Successful people have had to handle adversity, overcome challenges, and go over, under or through obstacles. And they most likely continue to do so today.

Here's a man who had tremendous challenges and adversity in his life. Can you guess who this is?

He failed in business.
He was defeated for state legislator.
He tried another business. It failed.
His fiancée died.
He had a nervous breakdown.
He ran for Congress and was defeated.
He tried again and was defeated again.
He tried running for the Senate. He lost.
The next year he ran for Vice-President and lost.
He ran for the Senate again and was defeated.
And then the man, who signed his name A. Lincoln,
was elected as the 16th President of the United States.

Abraham Lincoln obviously did not allow defeat to become permanent. He persevered, and in spite of challenges he rose above them and became the President of the United States.

It is your reaction to adversity that will make the difference. It is what you will do about it. Or, better still, it is what you will BE that will make the difference. Will you be determined? Will you be one who perseveres? Will you be optimistic, positive, enthusiastic, strong, and focused?

How do you handle challenges when they come along today? Do you give up easily, or do you see the opportunity in the situation?

* * * * * * * *

Are you ready for challenges when they come along? Are you prepared for adversity?

I'm sure you remember the story about the Three Little Pigs. In the story, each one of the pigs built a house to protect himself from the big bad wolf. The first pig made his house out of hay, the second pig made his house out of wood, and the third house was built by a smart Pig (a pig who had read *The 8 Proven Secrets to SMART Success*) and he built his house out of brick. He was a smart pig who was prepared.

The stronger you are, emotionally, psychologically, physically; the stronger your beliefs; the higher your level of confidence; the greater your faith – all of these things will make it easier for you to get through challenging times.

Elliott Smith is a friend of mine and a great performer, both as a magician and as a fire eater. One evening while he was in Montreal performing his fire-eating act, someone opened a door that let in a huge rush of wind, which caused the flames to explode in his face. He was burnt severely. Elliott, being the professional that he is, finished his act, and at the conclusion, immediately drove himself to the hospital. By the time he arrived at Emergency, the pain was so intense he almost passed out. They diagnosed him with second and third degree burns to his face and neck. He was wrapped up like a mummy and had to keep the bandages on his head for days. After one week, he went to his own doctor back home. When the doctor removed the bandages, he asked him when the accident had happened, expecting to hear "several weeks ago" as an answer. When Elliott said "one week ago," the doctor was in total disbelief. He said: "There is no way these scars are only one week old." The healing was far more advanced than that of a one-week-old accident. Elliott told the doctor that he believed the advanced healing was the result of his positive attitude and being in great physical condition. Elliott believes these are the two main causes for his fast recovery.

* * * * * * *

Elliott takes great care of his physical body and he is one of the most enthusiastic and positive men that I know. He has experienced fast recovery for other life challenges that he's been faced with, and he knows that his positive mental attitude helps him deal with anything that comes along.

Build your emotional muscles to be ready to easily and effectively handle adversity, challenges and obstacles.

Here are 5 simple-to-use, simple-to-apply keys that will help you manage through any challenge, obstacle or adversity:

1. Don't make it bigger than it is.
2. Look for the gift.
3. Learn from it.
4. Look past it.
5. Be relentlessly persistent.

Let's look at each one of these in greater detail:

1. Don't make it bigger than it is.
How many times have you seen someone lose a job, or a sale, or a boyfriend or girlfriend, or fail an exam, or lose some money, and the next thing you know, they feel as if their entire life is destroyed, or over? Has this ever happened to you?

A couple of years ago I received a call from a friend of mine. She was crying hysterically on the other end of the telephone. "My life is over!" she cried. I immediately thought that she had been diagnosed with some kind of incurable disease. I responded, with concern: "What happened?" She jumped in: "He left me. He left me. He's found someone else and he's gone!"

• • • • • • • •

I can empathize with the pain of the loss of a relationship and I believe people need to be in touch with those feelings and express them, AND get over them. First of all, her life was not over. It took only a few minutes to remind her of her own dissatisfaction with the relationship she had been in for the past two years. She just needed to take inventory of what was great with her life.

She had a great job; she was healthy, young, attractive, and financially independent. When she shifted her focus, she started to realize that her life wasn't over, as she had thought, and that she just needed to get over this relationship loss and not allow it to harm the other healthy parts of her life.

I've seen businesspeople lose their self-confidence because they lost their jobs. You are not your job. You have to know that when you lose your self-confidence everything in your life is affected. For example, a lack of self-confidence makes it far more difficult to get a new job, or keep healthy relationships with your loved ones and your friends. Loss of self-confidence will spread through your life like a virus and infect everything it touches.

The fact that you have lost your job doesn't mean you whole life is over. It simply means you have new career choices. There is opportunity everywhere and I mean everywhere. If you make it bigger than it is, you become completely blinded to new opportunities. You likely won't even go looking for them and when they show up in front of your face, you certainly won't see them.

Do not allow one challenging area of your life to spiral the other parts of your life downward.

Minimize the situation.

● ● ● ● ● ● ●

If your sales this month were the lowest or the year, just decide, "okay, that is going to be the lowest sales for the year and every other month I will surpass those results." If you start to think that sales are bad, the economy is going in the dumps or people aren't buying any more – you'll start to send energy in that direction and contribute toward the effect. Don't go there! One bad month in sales doesn't mean your entire year is ruined.

If you are having a bad month financially, don't focus on debt or lack. You'll create more of it. Focus on what you want to have happen; see yourself with financial prosperity, enjoying the financial independence that you desire. Don't join the ranks of the financially strapped. I once heard that the best thing you can do for the poor is not be one of them.

Don't let one low period knock you off track from your annual goals.

Don't let one bad relationship keep you from experiencing another totally fulfilling relationship.

Don't let a one person's opinion dictate who you are and what you are capable of achieving.

Quite often we blow things way out of proportion. Keep things in perspective and be SMART by engaging your common sense.

And just remember, everyone has challenges. Quite often we compare our own lives to others' and create a false belief that everyone else has it so much better than we have it. I'll always remember my good friend Anick saying to me: "If we hung our problems on our clothes line like we hang our laundry, everyone would be quickly running back to their own back yard." Maybe your problems aren't really as bad as you think they are.

> "I have often been afraid, but I would not give in to it. I made myself act as though I was not afraid and gradually my fear disappeared."
>
> – Theodore Roosevelt

2. Look for the gift.

Looking for the gift in adversity is sometimes difficult for people to grasp, but truly, in every adversity there is a seed of greatness.

A few years ago I did some work with the national Olympic Synchro swim team. One of the lessons I taught them was how to overcome challenges, obstacles and adversity. I recommended to the ladies to "look for the gift" in the adversity, and any time that they were faced with adversity, to ask themselves this question: What is great about this?

As usual, when I pose that question "what is great about this?" as it relates to adversity, I get very strange looks.

One of the young ladies on the Synchro team wrote me a letter seven months later. She said that she found my words truly valuable for her career and her personal life. And, at this time in her life, she found that question "comforting," as she was going through a huge personal loss, in that her father had just died unexpectedly of a heart attack.

In her letter, she said that she could hear me saying those words to her, and heard that question, "what is great about this?" Obviously, it isn't great that she lost her father – that is not what I'm saying, nor would I imply that in any way. She found the gift in the memories of her father and the close relationship that she had shared with him. With this shift in focus, she was able to manage through the pain with greater ease. She chose to focus on the great things about their meaningful father/daughter relationship and she'll cherish the memories forever.

* * * * * * * *

When my brother Gary died at the young age of 49, my entire family came together to mourn the loss. The pain was intense, especially for my parents, who had lost their child (and as my Mother said, "It doesn't matter how old he was, he was still our child . . . and there is no greater pain.")

Our relatives had flown in from all over the country. I recall sitting at the table with my other brother, sister-in-law, sister, mother, niece, and nephew, and we were laughing. We reminisced about the fun and joyful times we shared with Gary and we laughed so hard at some of the memories that our sides hurt. I couldn't remember ever laughing that hard. To see my Mom laughing was pure joy. I knew she hurt deeply inside, and to see her laugh was wonderful. It was at that moment that I could hear that question ringing in my own head: "What's great about this?" And I had my answer. It was great to have my family together. It was great to have such a wonderful, close and loving family, and it was great to be able to remember Gary with such fond and happy memories.

As difficult as it may be, when you are going through adversity or challenges of any kind, remember to always look for the gift. You'll find it when you look for it.

3. Learn from it.
Choosing to learn from challenging situations is one of the best things you can do for yourself. This will move you quickly from despair to optimism.

As soon as you are faced with adversity, at the precise moment it hits, ask yourself this:

What do I choose to learn from this?

There is a lesson in adversity; we can simply choose to learn from it. There is a possibility that we will become aware of our contribution to an undesirable result and choose not to repeat it in the future.

* * * * * * * *

You may also ask yourself: What is this experience revealing to me? What role have I played in creating this in my life? Were there signs to indicate that this was going to happen?

When you choose to learn from a situation, you choose to grow from it.

Remember to be aware.

Here are some additional questions to help you learn from challenges, obstacles and adversity:

What will I do differently next time?
What have I done in the past to get through this?
What have others done?
What strategies are most effective?
Is there another way?
How will I do this?
Who else has done this?
What resources are available?
What do I choose NOW?
What WILL I do today to take control of this situation?
How will I solve this now?

When you say "How will I . . . ?" you are using a pre-assumptive question. This type of question assumes that you will do something.

Ask the questions that get the results you desire.

4. Look past it.
Here's a technique that I've used countless times to get through challenging times. Repeat these words quietly in your mind: "This too shall pass."

● ● ● ● ● ● ● ●

"Being defeated is only a temporary condition; giving up is what makes it permanent."

– Marilyn vos Savant

There is so much truth in that statement. Being defeated is only temporary . . . UNLESS you make it permanent. Do not make it permanent; look past it. Look forward, or better yet, look up and you'll go up.

There is a reason why our Creator put our eyes in the front of our head – to look forward.

Have a positive attitude in light of your challenge.

Here are the words from the Power of Attitude Successories©️ Posters:

> "Our lives are not determined by what happens to us, but by how we react to what happens to us; not by what life brings to us, but by the attitude we bring to life. A positive attitude causes a chain reaction of positive thoughts, events and outcomes. It is a catalyst . . . a spark that creates extraordinary results."

Do you have words of wisdom, quotes, or any other sayings that really stay with you? Many, many years ago I heard this saying: "Don't cry over anything that won't cry over you." That has stayed with me for many years. If I ever feel my eyes well up with tears and I'm about to cry over something that I know for certain will not cry over me, I ask myself, "what will this solve?" If the answer is "nothing", then I choose happiness.

And, here is another old saying that has a lot of wisdom in it: *It is always darkest before the dawn.* Remember that it always appears to be darkest just before things start to get brighter. The sun will rise tomorrow, guaranteed. It may have set, but only for a brief period of time.

* * * * * * * *

"I don't let obstacles get me down. I focus on how to overcome them. You can work around any obstacle by going under it if it's too high, going over it if it's too low. There's always a way!"
– James "Rocky" Robinson

Successful people only see things working out.

Be aware that the solution to the problem is already there; you simply have to become aware of it, and it will reveal itself to you in time.

"Everything works out right in the end. If things are not working right, it isn't the end yet. Don't let it bother you; relax and keep on going."
– Michael C. Muhammad

5. Be relentlessly persistent

"For the resolute and determined there is time and opportunity."
– Ralph Waldo Emerson

Be the dog with a bone. I have a book on this topic alone called *On Being a Dog with a Bone*. It is a book about never giving up on your dreams.

I was inspired by my own childhood dog Pepe, who would get hold of a bone and not let go, no matter what. I believe you have to have this type of attitude to truly succeed.

Be persistent and, as Winston Churchill so eloquently said, "Never, ever, ever, ever give up."

If you see obstacles, go around them, over them, through them, under them. If you fall behind, push harder, go stronger, and be stronger than you were before. If some well-meaning person comes along and tries to push you off track, get right back on again. If you lose faith in your goal, get it back again. You had the faith before; you can get it again.

If you fall down, get back up. It isn't going down that is the challenge; the challenge is if you stay down. Don't stay down. Choose to get back up again.

Another Great Challenge

There is another great challenge that you will likely encounter on your journey through life, and that is the challenge of dealing with the internal chatter in your head. Dr. Shad Helmsttetter built his reputation around the topic of self-talk. He wrote a number of marvelous books on the subject, including a book called *What to Say When You Talk to Yourself.* He also wrote my personal favorite, The *Self Talk Solution.*

You see, inside your head there is dialogue occurring. Apparently, some studies show that on average 75 percent of the thoughts that people think are negative. I really wonder how these folks got inside people's heads to monitor that quiet self-talk, but if you think about it, and evaluate your own self-talk, you might conclude that they are fairly accurate.

We've talked about it before, and you'll hear about it again . . . *what you think about comes about.* Most people wish for something positive and think about what they don't want. Let me give you an example. Let's say a person has considerable debt, lives paycheck to paycheck, and barely squeaks by each month. They wish for financial independence and continually think about their debt. What they are doing is planting a seed, and uprooting it. They wish for something and then cancel it out by thinking about what they *don't* want. It's like planting a healthy seed and immediately putting weed killer on it.

● ● ● ● ● ● ● ●

THE **8** PROVEN SECRETS TO SMART SUCCESS

Here's where it gets even trickier. Let's say this person has become a goal-achieving, committed-to-personal-development kind of person. They are focused on their goal of financial independence; they have created powerful, positive goal statements, which they read every day; and they still continue to think about how they are going to pay their debts and engage in a state of being called *doubt*. This person may be doing some of the greatest creative things to change their life, but if they continue to doubt and think about debt and lack, they are planting and uprooting, planting and uprooting, planting and uprooting.

Why would anyone want to do this? Honestly, I don't think anyone would consciously choose to do this. My best guess is that this type of creation and destruction simply comes from not knowing, not being aware of the internal negative chatter and its effect.

As you go through your day, take note of your internal chatter. Is it positive or is it negative? Is it creative or is it destructive? Pay particular attention to it. Consciously choose to monitor your thoughts for an entire day. When you notice negative chatter, immediately put a stop to it and plant your "desire" seeds again. This can quite literally be the single area that has been blocking you or holding you back from living the life that you truly desire.

Thinking positive equals positive results. It is that simple!

Create your own strategies for handling adversity, getting through obstacles and overcoming challenges.

You can do it before, or you can do it after. I highly recommend that you prepare in advance. It is so much easier on you when you do.

Christopher Reeve is a man who has had to deal with extreme adversity and continual challenges. In 1995 a freak accident left him paralyzed from the neck down.

* * * * * * * *

He is now the Chairman of the Board of the Christopher Reeve Paralysis Foundation and the Vice-Chairman of the National Organization on Disability, and he lobbies vigorously for health-care reform and funding for research.

He is an example of possibility, and in his newest book, *Nothing Is Impossible*, he shares a story about a sailing experience that he had 17 years before his accident.

He tells the story about how he and three other men set off from Connecticut to sail to Bermuda on a 48-foot sloop. They expected a 4- to 5-day passage, but their voyage was beset by unexpected horrific weather challenges. A storm came upon them that scared them beyond words. It was only when they saw the faint light of the Gibb's Hill Lighthouse that they knew there was hope that they would make it alive. Here's an excerpt from Christopher's book:

> "At some time, often when we least expect it, we all have to face overwhelming challenges. We are more troubled than we have ever been before; we may doubt that we have what it takes to endure. It is very tempting to give up, yet we have to find the will to keep going. But even when we discover what motivates us, we realize that we can't go the distance alone.
>
> When the unthinkable happens, the lighthouse is hope. Once we find it, we must cling to it with absolute determination, much as our crew did when we saw the light of Gibb's Hill that October afternoon. Hope must be real, and built on the same solid foundation as a lighthouse; in that way it is different from optimism or wishful thinking. When we have hope, we discover powers within ourselves we may have never known – the power to make sacrifices, to endure, to heal and to love. Once we choose hope, everything is possible. We are all on this sea together. But the lighthouse is always there, ready to show us the way home."

Where is your chart taking you? Are you navigating your way to success? Are you prepared to battle those storms? Is your ship sturdy and able to handle the rugged weather?

Think about that. Make it easier for yourself to manage through challenging times by using these strategies. Be prepared and be ready to handle anything that comes your way by developing an optimistic and positive attitude of mind and the states of being of relentless persistence.

I'll close Secret 6 with a quote by Oliver Wendell Holmes:

> **"Greatness is not where we stand, but in what direction we are moving. We must sail sometimes with the wind and sometimes against it – but sail we must, and not drift, nor lie at anchor."**

* * * * * * * *

Secret Number 7:
Be a Student: Study Success

● ● ● ● ● ● ● ●

The 7th proven and, I'll add, powerful secret to success is to get hungry and stay hungry. Not for food, but for wisdom. Remember what I said in the beginning of this program?

Knowledge + understanding = Wisdom

So the 7th proven secret is:

BE A STUDENT: STUDY SUCCESS

If success is your choice, choose to be an eager student, one who is committed to constant and never ending growth.

Be hungry to learn. Learn everything you can about success, if you want to be successful. And, never, ever, ever, stop learning.

Be a proverbial sponge.

To stop learning or to think that you've got it all is the most dangerous thing you can do!

Your cup is never full. As soon as you think it is, you will stop the universal flow of intelligence. The moment you decide, "Okay, I've got it; I've learned everything I need to learn about this" there will be something else to learn.

● ● ● ● ● ● ● ●

Actually, you are not necessarily *learning*, you are heightening your awareness. You see, you already know all of this. There isn't anything new here. There are no great revelations. There are simply new understandings and new awareness of what we already know. You may simply have forgotten.

How do you accelerate, enhance and heighten your awareness? Here are the 8 Keys:

1. **Be open-minded**
2. **Sit in the front row**
3. **Be an observer**
4. **Seek for answers**
5. **Create the answers**
6. **Develop a learning curriculum and follow it**
7. **Learn from experiences a.k.a. mistakes**
8. **Be an expert**

Let's review each of these 8 keys in greater detail:

1. Be open-minded

This key is first for a reason. It is vitally important. One of the challenges that I experience as a coach, working with clients with limiting beliefs, is this. I help them determine their limiting beliefs, and they agree, but they do not accept new ideas that will create new empowering and positive beliefs. They hear the words, they agree with the words, but they don't let them in. They immediately reject the ideas because they are so stuck in their limited mindset. They are hearing the words and the words just bounce off like a rubber ball hitting a brick wall.

Consider this excerpt from my first book *On Being… The Creator of Your Destiny*:

> Non-supportive and limiting beliefs hold us back so that we cannot move forward in our life. Negative, non-supportive beliefs are destructive and can sabotage our ability to achieve

● ● ● ● ● ● ● ●

our goals. Being clear on what these destructive beliefs are gives us tremendous power. This allows us to face the beliefs that have been keeping us from our joy and happiness. A two-part saying applies well to beliefs: "what you resist, persists" and "what you look at, disappears."

Having limiting beliefs can also block our minds from allowing any new ideas or new possibilities to be considered. It is not a matter of not being able to accept more – we simply reject. Think of the metaphor of your mind as a bottomless container; you can always put more in and the container will never fill up. The limiting belief is like cellophane on top of your mind; when you try to pour more in, it simply won't go in.

Consider new possibilities when they are presented to you. I'm not saying that you have to let every possible idea into your head. You still need to engage your common sense, and that is what being SMART is all about.

Being open-minded will also help you immensely when you are faced with a confrontation with another individual. Consider another view. Relativity is based on beliefs. We, as humans, decide what is true or false, right or wrong, good or bad, based on our beliefs. And, from time to time, we will make a new decision based on new information. But you must first be open to the new information.

> **"Nothing is either good or bad, but thinking makes it so."**
> – *Hamlet*, **Shakespeare**

Make a choice to be open-minded. Make sure that you have a belief that you can learn. If your belief is "I just can't seem to get this," then you are blocking the flow. You are cutting off intelligence from being received in your conscious mind.

●　●　●　●　●　●　●　●

2. Sit in the front row

When you go to a seminar, training event, speaking engagement, or any other venue that is helping you learn more about your industry, personal development or any other valuable topic, sit in the front row or as close as you can get to the front of the room.

You will get far more out of an event when you are sitting in the front row.

To get a front row seat, you usually have to arrive early. If an event is scheduled to start at 8:30 a.m., arrive at 7:30 a.m. and place your notebook or some other personal item on the seat, to reserve your spot.

If the event you are attending is in a large ballroom and the doors are closed, walk in and act like you own the place. You'll be surprised that no one will stop you. If you walk into a closed room with trepidation, and you have that look that says you don't think you should be in the room, you will likely get thrown out. But when you walk in with confidence and certainty, walk right up to the front row, and place your personal belongings down, you'll give the impression that you belong there. Then, promptly leave the room. You have now reserved your spot at the front of the room.

I've attended events where you had to purchase priority or preferential seating. If this is the case, and this event is important to you, invest the extra money to sit at the front of the room. You will receive a higher return on your investment for doing so.

Make eye contact with the speaker/presenter. Let him know that you are listening intently. This will cause the speaker to feel the connection with the audience and he will be more enthusiastic.

When you are sitting at the front of the room you are less likely to be distracted by other participants. Your focus will be intensified because your primary attention is on the speaker and the presentation.

● ● ● ● ● ● ● ●

And while you are there, take plenty of notes. I have journals filled with notes from events that I have attended over the years, and they are valuable reference material for me. If you have a laptop computer, and it is appropriate, take it with you and type your notes. If an electrical outlet is available, plug your laptop in and you will be certain to have lots of power to keep your laptop charged in order to take notes for the entire day. This only works if you are a fast typist. If you cannot type, this technique may not work as well as writing notes. Either way, always take plenty of notes. Your memory will fade, but the ink will not.

3. Be an observer

You can learn a lot just by watching people. How can you use this? Let's say your goal is to reach a higher level of success in your business, industry or organization. Find the people who are getting the results that you want and watch them. Watch their mannerisms and body language. Communication is 55 percent body movements and gestures. Observe how they interact with others. If they exude confidence, observe how they stand, take note of their posture, watch how they walk, and examine their gestures.

One of the best-known methods to build rapport with another is to mirror their movements. If you are looking to build rapport with another, observe their body movements and mirror them. Don't be blatantly obvious, but mirror them with subtlety. An unconscious connection between you and the other person will be occurring and they won't even know it is going on. This works with the Law of Synchronicity, which basically states that when two objects are moving in the same direction at relatively the same speed they will start to take on characteristics of each other and begin to move together. Have you ever observed two people who have rapport walking down the street? Their pace is the same, their steps are the same, and usually their arm movements are the same. They are synchronized, walking in harmony.

● ● ● ● ● ● ● ●

Be a SMART observer by evaluating for yourself whether there is something of value that you can use to help you achieve greater success.

And when you do observe others, take what you can use, throw out the rest, and develop your own unique style.

4. Seek answers

Finding answers is easy when you decide to look for them. The world is filled with reference material and countless stories of people who have achieved extraordinary success. You can find wisdom in books, magazines, trade journals, on the Internet, or at your public library. Not having the money to buy the materials is no longer an excuse. There are thousands of public libraries in this world. You can even go to your public library and read for hours and not spend one red cent.

Every year thousands and thousands of new books are published and are overflowing with valuable and beneficial information just waiting for you to study.

My great teacher Bob Proctor used to say "A home without books is like a house without windows." Books expand our minds, open up our imagination, spark our enthusiasm and ignite our desires.

Read from great books: motivational, personal development, inspirational and spiritual books. Great and wise books are investments. When you invest in books you are investing in your life!

When you read a book, have a highlighter and a pen ready. Dog-ear the pages that have significant messages that you will want to refer to later. Do not just read the book; devour it. Take notes as you are reading. Transcribe your notes. Find ways to implement these great ideas in your life. Apply the wisdom that you are learning, and learn from the result of the application.

* * * * * * * *

My own personal library is filled with books that are dog-eared, highlighted and written in. I do not lend my books, as they are my reference library and I constantly refer to them. If a client or friend has a desire for a book in my library, rather then lending it, I will buy it for them as a gift. You'll quite often hear me say that if my house ever caught on fire, after everyone is safely out I would try to save my library next. My library is one of my most cherished properties.

Read magazines on the subject that interests you most. Read the trade magazines for your industry or the corporation magazines for your organization. Read the general interest magazines that may have a great story with something of value for you to learn to help you succeed.

Have fun while you are studying. You'll quickly determine your level of passion for a subject by the intensity of your studying. Do you look forward to reading a book on a specific subject? Are you eagerly signing up for seminars in a chosen field? Are you making financial investments in programs that help you deliver more value to others?

If you want to determine the subjects of greatest interest to you, take a look at the books that you read now and the magazines that you look through. This will give you a great idea of the subjects that interest you if you don't already know. Quite often one who is genuinely interested in romance will read romance novels and other love stories. Someone who is interested in automobiles may read trade magazines that highlight sports cars or auto trends. Or, if you are interested in sales, you may read magazines that teach you about selling, or offer valuable information about your market or potential market.

• • • • • • • •

A friend of mine is a President and CEO of an Internet technology firm and he invests a significant amount of time in the evenings, on weekends, or while traveling on airplanes reading articles from Internet-related magazines. This keeps him up to date with the market and the trends and gives him more knowledge to make the necessary decisions for his own company's direction. His heightened awareness gives him a higher profile because he is considered an "expert" in a highly evolving industry.

5. Create answers

Seeking answers is one thing; creating answers is quite another. When you are seeking answers, you are looking for the confirmation of what another has done before. When you are creating answers, you are entering new ground, an area where no man has gone before. This is where it gets a little tricky.

Basically, what I am saying here is this: if you have a desire to do something, or create something that has not been done before, you can create the answers and find the way.

> "The people who get on in this world are the people who get up and look for the circumstances they want, and if they can't find them, make them."
> – George Bernard Shaw

We could fill the pages of many books with stories about people who had a desire to do something, who were told by their loved ones, as well as others, that it couldn't be done, and who, regardless, made it happen.

Christopher Reeve has been mentioned earlier in this book. He is a great example of this kind of creativity. Based on his type of injury, he was told he would never be able to move any part of his physical body below a certain level. A few weeks ago I saw him on television demonstrating the movement of his finger. The one simple movement shocked the medical industry, as it had been assumed that he

• • • • • • • •

would never be able to do this. Christopher Reeve is committed 100 percent to walking again. Has anyone ever done that before with his type of injury? No, but he will not let that get in his way. He is committed to find the way, and I'm certain he will.

6. Develop a learning curriculum and follow it

Plan to go to school for the rest of your life. Attend the school of life. When we finish our formal education we are no longer part of a structured or formal learning curriculum. But does this mean that our education is complete? Absolutely not! Once you have decided on the profession, business or career of choice create your own learning curriculum and follow it.

What do I mean by that? Let's use an example of an industry that I am very familiar with, the independent sales industry. Here is an example of a structured learning curriculum for an individual committed to being successful in the sales industry:

- Read one new book a week. When I recommend this to people they are quite often shocked . . . "You want me to read one new book a week?" "Yes, that's right!" For the sake of this example, we'll use my first book *On Being...The Creator of Your Destiny.* This book is 184 pages. You can read this book in less than 2 hours. When you were in University, 2 hours would equal one class. Assume that you have one class each week and it is a reading class. Schedule it in and read the book. Or break it down and read for 30 minutes for 4 days and you'll be able to easily read at least one book each week.

- Listen to personal development, sales, audio tapes or CDs while you are in your car. If you only drive for 30 minutes each day, you can get 3.5 hours of study in each week while you are driving your car. You haven't added any extra hours of work to your week because you were already going to be driving. Now you will utilize this time as part of your structured learning curriculum.

● ● ● ● ● ● ● ●

- Listen to personal development, sales, audio tapes/CDs or audio books while you are taking public transportation. If you don't have a car, you can still listen to audio programs with a portable audio device such as a Walkman©.

- At the conclusion of each day, write down in a journal what you have learned that day. Also write down the things you will do as a result of your learning. This is where you take the wisdom and apply it.

- Flip through trade magazines during your lunch breaks. Carry magazines with you and go through them when you are waiting for an appointment or whenever you have a few minutes. Place your important magazines on your table or counter in the kitchen where they are visible and look at them in the evening after your meal, or place them on your coffee table in the living room and read them in the comfort of your home and at your leisure. If you put your magazines out of sight, they are out of mind.

- When you are traveling on vacation you can continue to learn. Bring a book with you to read on the airplane.

- Always carry a notebook or a journal with you and document ideas or strategies that you hear, read or simply think about that are most valuable to you and will help you succeed. Have a journal small enough that it is convenient for you to carry anywhere.

You'll be amazed at the number of learning activities that you can incorporate into your regular week without causing any major changes or adding to the workload. Developing and following a learning curriculum is implementing a new discipline, and like any new discipline it will become habitual and natural once you consistently engage in these new activities.

• • • • • • • •

7. Learn from experiences, a.k.a. mistakes

The word "mistake" is a word that should be replaced with the words "learning experiences." There is no such thing as mistakes; there are only learning experiences.

This may seem like a subtle semantic difference, but think about it for a minute. When you know that you have made a mistake, how does that make you feel? Your self image is weakened when you believe that you've made a mistake. However, if you have had a learning experience, which implies that you've learned something as a result of an experience, your self-image is strengthened.

Early in my career I accepted a position in a computer firm as a product manager writing product manuals for the marketing department. My previous business experience involved working with clients as a customer services representative. Working with people was something that I loved to do. What I didn't realize at the time was that working in a back room writing product manuals was a job that was going to be completely inappropriate for me.

I enthusiastically accepted the position and went to work. As the first week at my new job came to an end, I realized that I had made a big mistake. I was in a job that was completely unsuited to me. I didn't know what to do. I had just started this job. How could I quit now . . . after only one week? I decided to stick with it.

The days at the office were really long. I despised getting up in the morning. I hesitate to use this word, but I *hated* my job. My distaste for my job started to come through in my work. My work was no longer superior, but inferior. I was losing my self-confidence, and my lack of confidence was evident in my work. My belief was that I needed to put in a few years with my new employer, or else I would appear to be a non-committed employee to potential future employers.

I'm certain you can guess what happened. After two months I was fired. Now I was out of a job and my self-confidence had really taken a beating. At the time, I was devastated. Looking back, it was one of the best things that could have ever happened to me. That was a career learning experience for me. It was obvious to me where my best talents could be utilized, and it was not in a back room writing manuals.

When you experience situations such as this and you believe you have made a mistake, learn from it. See the gift in every experience, because it is there. Every so-called mistake has a valuable lesson contained within it. You only need to be aware of it, learn from it and move forward. You will be that much wiser as a result.

Have you ever heard the comment "One day we'll laugh at this"? My recommendation is to laugh at it *now*. If you know you are going to laugh at it in the future, you may as well laugh at it now. Maintain your sense of humor when you have those so-called "learning experiences." Engaging your sense of humor will also help you see the value in the lesson.

8. Be an expert
If you have a goal to be a successful business person, learn everything you can about being a success in the business you are in and be recognized as the one who is the most knowledgeable.

If your goal is to have a healthy, loving and fulfilling relationship, become an expert on building a healthy, loving and fulfilling relationship.

If your goal is to be an outstanding parent, become an expert on being the best parent you can possibly be.

If your goal is to be in top physical condition, become an expert on health, fitness and nutrition.

● ● ● ● ● ● ● ●

Learn everything you can about your industry, your products, your competitors and, most importantly, the benefits you bring to others. People do not make buying decisions based on products or services; they invest because they believe they will receive a benefit.

Do not assume anything. Become an expert at finding out what your customer's motives are. Discover how they evaluate and make buying decisions.

Learn everything you can about your customers. Find out the SMART information. The SMART information is the valuable information, not useless information. When you learn everything about your customer, he or she believes you care and, actually, you do care. People don't care how much you know until they know how much you care.

People don't care how much you know until they know how much you care.

Learn everything you can about your children. What are their dreams, what are their favorite colors, favorite foods, favorite memories and their interests?

Learn everything you can about your life partner: their dreams, their desires, and their challenges.

Be an expert in your industry. Learn everything you can about your business. Be the resource person for others to go to when they need assistance. Willingly share the knowledge that you have acquired.

Be an expert on the subject of you. Learn everything you can about your strengths and your weaknesses. Focus your efforts on building those strengths and managing your weaknesses. Your strengths are the areas where you have innate talent. To turn a talent into a strength, you have to work at it.

● ● ● ● ● ● ● ●

And, as you are striving to be the expert in your field, never, ever get clogged up with thinking you are an expert. The thought that you know it all will reject any additional information, or additional knowledge, and you will limit yourself. When people believe they have reached the "know it all" level, they start to lose it all. You are either growing or dying. Nothing in this universe stays the same, including you. Even though you may be considered the expert in the field, commit to constant improvement.

World champion athletes know that when they reach the number 1 spot in their sport, they must work just as hard or harder to stay there. There are numerous athletes right behind them with the same desire, to be the best, and they are working extremely hard to take that top position away.

While I was attending a book marketing session for authors at the Maui Writer's Conference in Hawaii, I turned around and noticed a familiar man sitting in the audience. It was Jack Canfield. Jack is the Co-Creator of the best selling series *Chicken Soup for the Soul*®. At the time of this conference Jack's book series had sold over 80 million copies and was listed in the Guinness Book of World Records as the most books sold in a series. After the session I asked Jack: "Why were you attending a book marketing session?" He responded, "The same reason as you – to learn."

Here was a man who was already extremely successful in the book marketing area. As a matter of fact, Jack was at the Maui Writer's Conference to speak on book marketing, and still, he invested the time to attend other events to see what he could learn.

So, you see, school didn't end at Grade 12 or once you were handed that degree. You are enrolled in the School of Life. Enjoy yourself in this learning environment, as it is extremely fulfilling.

* * * * * * * *

Stay open and stay a beginner.

Studying success is making an investment in your future. "Pay attention to the future, because that is where you are going to spend the rest of your life."

This thing called success is a lifetime commitment.

"We are what we repeatedly do. Excellence, then, is not an act, but a habit."
— Aristotle

Secret Number 8:
Be a Master

● ● ● ● ● ● ● ●

The first secret and the eighth secret of this book are the great bookends for the entire program. The first secret is to be aware and now, the 8th proven secret to SMART Success is:

BE A MASTER

Training to be a world-class athlete encompasses "mastering the fundamentals," which means doing the little things, little distinctions over and over and over again and making it a little better each time. It may be time-consuming and unglamorous, but nonetheless it is necessary.

Training to be a success in any area of your life follows the same requirement: you must master the fundamentals. Not some of them, or a few of them, but ALL of them. Reaching mastery is like orchestrating a symphony to play a masterpiece with perfection. Many instruments are required, and each and every instrument is played with the same precision and exactness. If one instrument is left out, the result is not the same. If one instrument is played off key, the total result is negatively affected. The same applies with your life and with these proven strategies to success.

If you desire a totally successful and fulfilling life, then master all of the secrets to success found in this book.

● ● ● ● ● ● ● ●

Here are the 4 keys to assist you to become a Master:

1. **Elevate your consciousness to a high level.**
2. **Help others be Masters.**
3. **Be a Master by example.**
4. **Unconditionally give to others.**

Let's understand each one of these in greater detail.

1. Elevate your consciousness to a high level.

When you are a master you have reached the stage of knowing. A master is at peace, calm and tranquil. Knowing is the state of being of absolute certainty and, might I add, masters achieve this state of certainty with humility. This is a wondrous place to be. It is here, in this place of knowing, that you accept whatever shows up for you in your life, and you accept it with gratitude. Instead of having expectations, requirements or addictions to certain results, you have acceptance. Because you know the perfect outcome is occurring. You seek results and outcomes, but do not require them.

This may sound like a paradox considering the 2nd secret, so let me explain further.

Earlier in the 2nd secret to SMART Success you set your intentions by setting pre-determined goals in all areas of your life. In secret number 8, you will continue to seek your results and outcomes, but now you are detaching yourself from the outcome. You have specified that you would like those things to show up and you are seeking them; however, you now realize that the perfect outcome always occurs. You may not be able to explain it, but nonetheless, the perfect outcome happens and you *know* it.

When I first ventured into this world of personal development and started to set clearly defined goals, stayed focused on my goals, and did the things that, I thought, successful people did, my life still wasn't the way I desired it to be. That was very frustrating, and then

• • • • • • • •

my awareness opened up and I started to hear this phrase "detach yourself from the outcome," and it was about that time that I became confused. Confusion was a benefit because it caused me to seek to understand.

When your consciousness has been elevated to this place of knowing, you simply know that the perfect thing will occur. Not that a particular thing will occur, but the *perfect* thing will occur. This is also called "letting go and letting God."

You always have the gift to choose your own outcomes, to create and experience your reality. The secret to life is to not having everything you want but to want everything you have. You may want to read the previous sentence again.

Therefore, it is true that there are no results that are unintended, but they may be unanticipated.

It is advisable to live your life without expectations. In every circumstance, in every situation, event or outcome, see the perfection, because each perfect outcome is designed to move you to a higher state of awareness to seek to become a master. So do not reject any part of your life, because if you do, you are rejecting a part of yourself.

2. Help others be Masters.

This is one of the greatest secrets in the universe, and it is so simple to understand. Do you realize that if you help another become a master, as a result, you will become a master? Masters have the highest calling – to be of service to others.

Here's the key: decide what you want, find another who seeks the same result, and teach them how to achieve it. In other words, let's say your desire is to be successful (and this may be safe to assume since you have picked up and invested in this book): find another who seeks the same, and teach them how to be successful.

● ● ● ● ● ● ● ●

There are 10 things that you can do to help another be a Master.

- Help them understand the creative ability that they possess.
- Help them understand the Universal Laws of the Universe.
- Help them find their true passion.
- Help them get clear on their desires (goals).
- Help them become a master who helps others be masters.
- Help them through challenging situations.
- Help them see the perfection of every result.
- Help them build the states of being of a successful individual.
- Help them grow every day and be the best that they can be.
- Help them be in the state of being of *knowing*.

"You cannot teach a man anything; you can only help him to find it within himself."

– Galileo

As a master you show others the way to mastery. Have this as your mantra: "Let me show you the way."

3. Be a Master by example.

If you have a child, or if you ever were one (which is pretty certain), you will understand this well. Your children are watching everything that you do. Children will mirror the behavior of their parents by observing, regardless of what the parents say. A parent may have a cigarette in their hand and say to their child "don't smoke," and when their teenager starts smoking, they say: "I told you not to smoke!" What did the parent expect? The child simply learned by example.

● ● ● ● ● ● ● ●

You are not invisible or transparent. People are watching you at all times, even when you least expect it. If you knew that another was going to walk the same path as you, would you take the path that you were planning to take today?

Teach others to be Masters by being a phenomenal enlightened Master; the example of who and what a Master is. People will emulate you.

> **"Example is not the main thing in influencing others.**
> **It is the only thing."**
> – Albert Schweitzer

Be a Master in your home, when you are with a group of friends, on a sports team, and/or in business. Regardless of whether you are "in charge" or not, you can still play a Master's role. The same applies for a sports team, even though you may not wear the "C" for Captain on your team: take the opportunity to play a Master's role on the team.

Here are the 10 things you can do to be a Master by example:

- Be the source of faith (at home, at the office, for your customers, for your team, with your family and friends) and help build faith in others.

- Be the one who directs the focus and keeps the focus where it needs to be (on the priorities).

- Be a pillar of strength and an undeniable representation of unwavering courage, demonstrating to others how to be strong and courageous. Turn pessimism into optimism.

- Bring everyone together to collaborate and find solutions engaging the tremendous creative power of a group of people.

• • • • • • • •

- Be an outstanding communicator. During good times and challenging times, communication is important and must be maintained. Make it your responsibility to ensure the communication is flowing and positive.

- Encourage others. Look for the positive qualities and strengths in others, and acknowledge them. Help others recognize their great qualities and to see the great gifts in adversity and the positive side to every situation.

- Reminds others of what is most important (values like integrity, honesty, love). Remind them of their purpose or the purpose of the team/business/family/group.

- Set the velocity and pace for others. Show others how to make things happen in record time.

- Be the voice of reason with calm assurance and turn a chaotic situation into a peaceful condition.

- Handle all challenges and adversity in a timely manner and show others how to do the same.

All of these points will help you become a Master. When you are a Master, you will benefit and so will so many others who happen to be in your presence.

Here's a great truth: "A true master is not the one with the most students, but one who creates the most masters." Become a master teacher, not to create followers, but to create other masters.

4. Unconditionally give to others.
A few years ago I was hosting a "live" seminar entitled Achieve Your Goals. The admission price for the seminar was $397. People from many different vocations signed up for this seminar. One evening I was quietly working in my office and the telephone rang. It was a

young woman by the name of Angie, expressing her sincere interest in the upcoming seminar. She had just read about the seminar in the newspaper. She asked about the contents of the seminar, and inquired into what she would get out of the seminar by attending. By the end of the conversation she was firmly convinced that she needed to be there. She only had one challenge: she didn't have the money to pay for her admission. Ironically, her primary reason to attend was because of her lack of funds and the challenges and dissatisfaction that it caused her in her life, and her desire to change that.

Angie had been recently divorced and was raising two young girls. Her ex-husband had left town and she was bore the sole responsibility for all of the expenses of her household; she had barely enough money to get by. She knew she needed to attend this seminar, and had a deep desire to do so, but could not make the financial investment.

I knew that Angie was an honest lady, as I could hear the sincerity in her voice. I told her I wanted to help. I offered her a complimentary ticket to attend the seminar. She was elated! She asked me how she could repay me. My response to her was to not be concerned with repaying me for the seminar as it was my pleasure and privilege to provide her with a free pass. I was firm that there was nothing that she needed to do as there were no expectations; the ticket was a gift. However, if she did want to do something, she could always pass it on.

She was puzzled and said: "What do you mean . . . pass it on?" I told her to come to the seminar with her own outcome – what she wanted to get out of the seminar – and after the seminar find another who had the same or a similar desire (to make positive changes in their life, one way or another) and help them with the knowledge that she would gain by attending the event. Angie agreed.

* * * * * * *

Angie enthusiastically attended the seminar. She sat in the front row, took lots of notes, and thanked me. I never heard from her again, nor did I have any expectations that I would, although I have thought about her from time to time and wondered how she is doing.

A few years later, I received a thank you card in the mail from a person named Sandra whom I had never met. In her card she stated that she had been a neighbor of a young woman who attended my Achieve Your Goals seminar a few years earlier (Angie). She told me that Angie was so excited about all she learned in that one day that she shared it with her neighbor. At the time, Sandra was also a single Mom and experiencing her own financial challenges, and as a result of her neighbor sharing in the strategies that she learned at the Achieve Your Goals Seminar, Sandra had managed to get herself completely out of debt and bought a brand new car with cash! In some way, she felt that I had helped her and wanted to send a special thank you. You see, Angie did pass it on, and another individual was able to benefit from Angie's commitment.

Generate ways that you can help another and do it without expectation of something in return. You may want to be sure that the other person wants the help. You remember that old adage, "You can lead a horse to water, but you can't make him drink." So lead the horse to water and then motivate him to drink.

And while you are doing great things for others, don't keep an account of the things that you have given to another. If you can't give unconditionally, don't give at all.

When people give with conditions they have expectations, and set themselves up for disappointment. This also creates a tension or strain on a relationship. When you give in a relationship, do so without expectation or conditions. If you have no expectation, and there are no conditions, there is no chance for disappointment.

* * * * * * * *

THE **8** PROVEN SECRETS TO SMART SUCCESS

"People who do things that count, never stop to count them."

The natural occurrence of unconditionally giving to another is that, whether you realize it or not, you are helping yourself.

"It is one of the most beautiful compensations of this life that no man can sincerely try to help another without helping himself."
– Ralph Waldo Emerson

In every endeavor and in all of your relationships (personal and business) do not seek what you will get; seek what you can give.

And here's a great method to create a prosperity consciousness. Give unconditionally even when you believe that you don't have enough. If money is a challenge, or lack of money is the challenge, my recommendation is to give away a portion of your money. Give some of it away even if it is only a single-digit percentage. And, more importantly, give it freely, with joy and without conditions.

A prosperous mind knows that there is an abundance of wealth in this world and there is always enough. When you do this, there is a natural flow in the universe that will cause money to be returned to you, but you must have faith – not expectation, but faith, a knowing that there is a universal flow of abundance. Being doubtful will push prosperity away; certainty will draw it to you like an intensely powerful magnet.

Look for ways that you can contribute to the lives of others. Contribute your time, your ideas, your products and your services. There are unlimited ways that you can contribute to the lives of others and do so without condition. Do it because you love to help.

* * * * * * *

Live your life beneficially! Live your life so that it benefits everyone you come in contact with. Touch people's lives in a special way. Make a positive difference in another's life. Ensure that another person's life is enriched when they create a union with you.

Mastery is reached when you have total freedom. That freedom includes the freedom of choice. Give yourself the freedom to make any choice you wish, and give those you love the same freedom. In Mastery you make choices based on what you believe is true for you, rather than what others have told you is truth or what society has decided is truth or what you think another would choose.

Choose to be a Master of your destiny.

● ● ● ● ● ● ● ●

Conclusion

● ● ● ● ● ● ● ●

How do you climb a mountain? One step at a time. Take this SMART Success program one step at a time. Don't look at the mountain and get overwhelmed or try to climb the whole thing at once.

The first law of learning is repetition. Read this book again and apply all of these important points daily until they are firmly embedded into your being.

Life is a process of creation. Every day you are creating. Every day is fresh, a clean slate, an opportunity to create or re-create. What do you choose? Do you seek success? Then create success in your life.

My great friend William E. Bailey says: "Totality requires totality. If you wish a total result you must give a total effort. It requires total focus, total determination, total courage and total vision."

If you desire a big result, you will need to make a big investment. Life is like a bank account: you can't make withdrawals unless you've made the deposits.

Master these disciplines. When you do, you will act as a young and enthusiastic child – you will start to do things spontaneously and innocently. It's almost as if you are ignorant (ignorant meaning not knowing) but, in fact, you are so aware that your innocence is bliss.

● ● ● ● ● ● ●

Everything you need is within you now.

"We've got to quit searching frantically for a Deity outside of ourselves and quietly listen to the one speaking within us."
– Albert Schweitzer

Your seeds of greatness were planted when you were born. A farmer whose seeds are planted in the fields already has his crop; he just hasn't seen the physical evidence of it yet. So, too, when you nurture the greatness within you, you will reap a marvelous harvest.

Create a perfectly orchestrated symphony for your life. The whole of *The 8 Proven Secrets to SMART Success* is greater than the sum of all parts. Blend it together to create a masterpiece – your beautiful and completely fulfilling successful life.

Wishing you a phenomenally successful and totally joyful life!

Peggy McColl

www.destinies.com

• • • • • • • •

Tools for Success available at
www.destinies.com

On Being...The Creator of Your Destiny Hard Cover Book
$29.95 Canada/$19.95 USA

The 8 Proven Secrets to SMART Success Soft Cover Book
$18.95 Canada/$12.95 US
Discover these amazing secrets that reveal how you can achieve an abundance of success and soar to new heights of prosperity! The 8 Proven Secrets to SMART Success is simple, practical and immediately beneficial! Your life will be transformed when you apply these powerful proven strategies.
Call for special pricing for bulk purchases 1-866-662-3464

The 8 Proven Secrets to SMART Success Audio Program.
$97.00 Canada/$67.00 US
This 4 audio CD program will step you through The 8 Proven Secrets to SMART Success book, workbook AND the e-course.

The 8 Proven Secrets to SMART Success Workbook
$34.97 Canada/$24.97 US
Based on the proven success methods found in the phenomenal book The 8 Proven Secrets to SMART Success, this workbook is a step-by-step guide to empower you to achieve all of your goals.

● ● ● ● ● ● ● ●

Create Your Ultimate Destiny CD
$24.97 Canada/$19.97 US
Not enough time to read the book? Would you like to spend productive time in the car? Are you looking for the inspiration to lift you into action? If so, the Create Your Ultimate Destiny audio CD is designed just for you! 34 minutes

Product Bundle
$67.00 Canada/$47.00 US

1. The 8 Proven Secrets to SMART Success Workbook.
Based on the proven success methods found in the phenomenal book The 8 Proven Secrets to SMART Success, this workbook is a step-by-step guide to empower you to achieve all of your goals.

2. On Being...The Creator of Your Destiny Hard Cover Book.
This book is written for those who want to take control of their life and create their ultimate destiny.

3. Create Your Ultimate Destiny CD.
Not enough time to read the book? Would you like to spend productive time in the car? Are you looking for the inspiration to lift you into action? If so, the Create Your Ultimate Destiny audio CD is designed just for you!

To purchase, go to http:/www. destinies.com

• • • • • • • •

References

Nothing is impossible: Reflections on a New Life
Christopher Reeve
ISBN 0-375-50778-8
Random House

The Man Who Tapped The Secrets of the Universe
Glenn Clark
ISBN 1-879-60507-4
University of Science and Philosophy

The Self-Talk Solution
Shad Helmstetter
ISBN 0-671-70882-1
Simon & Schuster Inc.

You'll See It When You Believe It
Dr. Wayne W. Dyer (audio program)
0-671-50592-0
Nightingale-Conant Corporation

● ● ● ● ● ● ● ●

About the Author

Peggy McColl has been a featured speaker throughout Canada and the United States. Whether as a keynote conference speaker or booked for a corporation seminar, Peggy combines a depth of knowledge of her material with an unparalleled level of enthusiasm.

Peggy McColl gives power-seeking people the proven framework to define and conquer their goals, then recognize and reach their maximum potential.

Author of the phenomenally selling books *On Being . . . The Creator of Your Destiny, The 8 Proven Secrets to SMART Success* and *On Being a Dog With a Bone*, sold and distributed in over 24 countries in the world, Peggy is also the Founder and President of Dynamic Destinies Inc., where she has developed the powerful Goal Management Achievement Planning System (GoalMAPS) – the most compelling and strategic goal system of its kind.

Peggy has more than 20 years of senior-level management experience in the high technology industry. Clients include Bell, Jaguar, Shell, Ericsson, the Department of National Defence and a number of Olympic teams.

Here's how to contact Peggy:
peggy@destinies.com   www.destinies.com

Dynamic Destinies Inc.
1 Stafford Road, Suite 312, Nepean, Ontario, Canada K2H 1B9
(613) 299-5722 in Ottawa
or toll free at 1-866-OnBeing (1-866-662-3464)

• • • • • • • •